PRESBYTERIANS, Their History and Beliefs

PRESBYTERIANS

Their history and beliefs

by
WALTER L. LINGLE
and
JOHN W. KUYKENDALL

John Knox Press
ATLANTA

Library of Congress Cataloging in Publication Data

Lingle, Walter Lee, 1868–1956.
  Presbyterians, their history and beliefs.

  1. Presbyterian Church—History. 2. Presbyterian-
ism. I. Kuykendall, John W., joint author.
II. Title.
BX8931.2.L56   1978   285   77–15750
ISBN 0–8024–0985–5

  10 9 8 7
Copyright © 1944, 1960, Revised edition 1978, 1988 John Knox Press
Printed in the United States of America

Foreword
to the
Fourth Revised Edition

The decision to produce a new edition of **Presbyterians, Their History and Beliefs** fifty years after its first appearance is a strong indication of its continuing value. Walter Lingle's original book, which has passed through several revisions and printings, was noteworthy for its winsome and uncomplicated presentation of the Presbyterian heritage. T. Watson Street's thorough revision was published in 1960. The present edition is intended to retain that attractiveness and simplicity, while incorporating information derived from current sources and events. In several instances, recent changes have necessitated the reframing of major portions of the text.

It would be nice to imagine that Dr. Lingle, with his avid but open appreciation of the Presbyterian way of life, would give his hearty approval to the ways in which the text has been reshaped to meet the circumstances of the present day. It would be equally satisfying to believe that this revised volume could have a fraction of the influence upon the life of the church which the older volume enjoyed.

A major aspect of my personal interest in this project has been my fond recollection of Dr. Lingle's daughter, the late Nan R. Lingle, who was my counselor, confidante, and friend during the years I spent in Davidson. My efforts in this enterprise are dedicated to her memory.

JOHN W. KUYKENDALL

Auburn, Alabama
November 1, 1977

JOHN CALVIN
1509-1564

Minister of the Word of God, Geneva
Theologian, Preacher, Pastor, Churchman

Contents

Chapter One

THE PRESBYTERIAN
INHERITANCE

Our Common Heritage

Christianity has sometimes been likened to a mighty tree, which has its roots deeply implanted in the rich soil of the faith experience of ancient Israel and emerges from a strong single trunk into a timber of great breadth and diversity. The Old Testament rootage provides us with a unique vision of God—a God who not only created us, but cares for us and is active in the events of history to work out our story in the way he intends. For Christians, the high point of that story comes in God's revelation of himself to us in the person of Jesus Christ.

The life, death, and resurrection of Christ is the seed from which the movement known (at first quite derisively) as "Christianity" emerged in the first century A.D. The seedling plant was endangered from the first by adverse conditions both within and without, but God's care brought it through the sapling stage with a remarkable degree of strength. The tree forked in the eleventh century, East and West; the western fork branched again in the sixteenth, Protestant and Catholic; and the Protestant fork has been constantly proliferating branches and twigs ever since.

The diversity of this flourishing organism has often been a source of amazement or distress—or both—to many who claim the name "Christian" for themselves. And it has frequently seemed more important to some believers to identify and validate the distinctiveness of their own branch or twig than to celebrate the life of the whole tree. As

Christians in the latter-twentieth century, we can be thankful that we live in a time in which such contentiousness is largely a thing of the past. Events of recent years have provided us with new possibilities for cooperation and communion with Christians who find themselves elsewhere on the family tree.

At the same time, we will be impoverished if we lose sight of the part of the story that is uniquely our own. Presbyterians—and Baptists and Lutherans and Roman Catholics—who cannot say why they are thus called, and what it is that makes them distinctive, typically contribute to the deadness of the tree rather than its life. Thus a book such as the present volume needs to be written, read, and digested; and though we ought never forget the ties we have to the rest of those in our world who claim the name of Christ, we can benefit from learning our own heritage and participating in its legacies.

Our Name and Our Origins

The first generation of Christian believers combined a lively expectation of the imminent return of Jesus with a fervent desire to spread his story as widely as possible in the Roman world. As the book of Acts shows us, men like Paul took up Jesus' commission to be his "witnesses . . . to the end of the earth" (Acts 1:8), and founded little cluster-communities of Christian believers wherever they could.

In most instances, the precise methods used in founding and organizing these infant congregations are hidden beneath the surface of the New Testament narrative. Occasionally, though, a term for the leaders of a local congregation occurs which is of more than passing interest to those who call themselves "presbyterian" over nineteen centuries later. It is interesting, of course, because it is the Greek word *presbyteros* from which we derive the name for our denomination.

This word occurs about sixty times in the New Testament and about a hundred times in the Greek translation of the Old Testament. It means "elder," and sometimes it is used simply to designate the older members of the community, who deserve the respect and attention of the rest of the community because of their years of experience and faithfulness. In other instances, however, the term seems to be used in more specialized fashion to designate a particular office of leadership, both in the Old Testament congregation and in the New Testament church. We read in Acts 20:17f., for example, that Paul holds a meeting with the "elders" of the church at Ephesus as he makes a stop at Miletus, in order to give them parting instructions concerning the care of their home congregation. Again, in the so-called Pastoral Epistles (1 and 2 Timothy and Titus), we find mention of the basic qualities of life which are expected of church officers, including those who have been chosen to serve as "elders." Literally speaking, then, a "presbyterian" church is a church governed by "elders," or, if we may expand a bit, it is a church with a representative form of government by elders elected by the people.

From time to time—at least since the Protestant Reformation in the sixteenth century—it has been argued that a representative form of government such as this was the only mode of organization which was used in the early church, and that any other form is merely a corruption of the original pattern. If modesty has not forestalled this argument in recent times, perhaps a lack of conclusive evidence has! Most students of the New Testament now agree that we do not have sufficient information there to determine precisely what form of organization is presumed by the writers of that document. It has been very persuasively argued, furthermore, that in all likelihood there was no one single mode of church government that was universal in apostolic times. Probably various sectors of the church used differing organizational styles, at least for a while. Thus the question of the origins of "presbyterianism" becomes a very complicated question indeed. Clearly the term itself is biblical, and there seems to be some evidence that government by elders does occur in some churches in the first century A.D.. However, we cannot claim scriptural warrant for the idea that ours is the only divinely ordained system, nor should those who hold to any other mode of organization.

In our day, presbyterianism is one among three well-known and widely practiced forms of church government, each of which can adduce some scriptural evidence for its existence. Most of us are already aware of the other two traditions, since they are used by Christian neighbors close at hand. One of them is the congregational form, in which all questions are decided in each local church by the membership of that congregation. Baptist and Congregationalist churches use this form of government. Each congregation is the final arbiter of its own affairs; no decisions which are made by denominational bodies or individual leaders can be considered binding upon a local church against its will.

The other traditional form of government, of course, is given the name "episcopal," deriving from the Greek word which means "overseer." It is also from this word that we get our English word "bishop," and churches having people designated to that office, such as the Roman Catholic, Episcopal, and Methodist churches, are all properly termed "episcopal" churches. After the first century, the episcopal form of government was clearly dominant in the early church, and eventually the use of the presbyterian mode (and the congregational, too) passed from the scene for a time. Before we discuss the revival of presbyterianism, we should briefly survey the developments which took place in the intervening generations of the church's life.

The Early Christian Community

Modern Christians who read the Acts of the Apostles are invariably impressed by the fervor and commitment of the first generation of followers of Jesus as they sought to share the gift of the gospel message with all who would listen. It is no less important to note that the early zeal of those disciples was broadened and deepened with the passage of time. Although their expectations of the immediate return of Christ subsided somewhat with the passage of the first decades after the Resurrection, their enthusiasm for spreading the faith to the rest of the world did not. Christianity made considerable headway during the first two or three generations of its existence, especially among the "classes and masses" of the urban centers of the empire, such as Ephesus, Corinth, and Rome.

As the new movement progressed, there were problems aplenty, both internal and external. The shadows of some of these difficulties fall across the pages of the New Testament. The matter of the relation of Christianity to Judaism, for example, was an issue of great concern for Paul and his colleagues in the Gentile mission. Eventually, in the so-called Jerusalem Conference (Acts 15), it was determined that the church was not bound to the legalistic traditions of the Old Testament, but only to the expression of God's grace in Jesus Christ as a means of salvation. Thus it became clear, once for all, that the Christian movement was not simply a sect of Judaism.

Further challenges were provided by the introduction of alien ideas and beliefs into Christian teaching, so that, even before the last document of our New Testament was penned, there was the necessity of warning Christians against false teachers *within* the church. Local congregations began to develop creedal statements (such as our Apostles' Creed, which is a later version of an early Roman baptismal affirmation) in order to insure a proper understanding of the faith on the part of all members. As time passed, the books that we now call the New Testament were gathered and accorded *canonical* or authoritative status as a means of bearing true witness to Christian belief.

Another development within the early church as it dealt with the growth-pains of the first generations of its life was the standardization of its pattern of organization. As in any other institution, the Christian community seems to have sensed the need for structural predictability. From its earlier diversity there began to emerge a uniformity of structures, focusing increasingly upon one person in each community to whom the title *bishop* was accorded. It is probable, at least in the beginning, that each bishop presided over only one local congregation, and the extent of his authority may have varied from place to place. Eventually, though, bishops came to hold authority over all the congregations in a given community and its immediate surroundings. Naturally, a bishop in a major urban center of the ancient world would thus come to occupy a position of greater responsibility than one in a relatively unsettled area, since his *diocese* or region of control would contain more churches and more Christians.

The importance of the episcopal office was further enhanced by the connection which came to be presumed between the apostles of the New Testament church and the bishops of later generations. Cyprian, the bishop of Carthage who was martyred in 258 A.D., expounded this idea of *apostolic succession.* He believed that the apostles were bishops themselves, that they had ordained other bishops who in turn had ordained others, and so on in unbroken succession down through the centuries. This succession was believed to be a guarantee that the true faith had been accurately passed from generation to generation. Cyprian even went so far as to say, "The bishop is in the church, and the church in the bishop, and if anyone is not with the bishop he is not in the church."

With the passage of time, the bishops of the more important communities came to take precedence over their colleagues in the lesser communities nearby, and thus the rank of *archbishop* or *metropolitan* bishop emerged. After awhile, five metropolitan bishops came to be called by the title *patriarch,* which set them in a place of special priority. The bishops of Rome, Constantinople, Alexandria, Antioch, and Jerusalem were accorded this title. Finally, the patriarchs of Rome and Constantinople came to be considered rivals for preeminence in Christian affairs, and eventually each would lead one segment of the East-West division which took place in the eleventh century.

Thus the structure of the Christian community emerged in a pattern which is usually identified as the *monarchical episcopate.* Each bishop was responsible for the oversight of his own diocese, and he also occupied a station in the hierarchy of bishops in the catholic or worldwide community.

The Church and the Roman Empire

The problems of doctrine and organization which beset the church from within were certainly not the only things about which early Christians had to worry. The situation of their growing community relative to the authority of the mighty Roman Empire was also a matter of constant concern. Jesus, after all, had been put to death with the consent of Roman authority, and the early generations of his followers learned that discipleship often meant "imitation of Christ" even to the extent of sharing the sort of physical persecution which he had undergone.

From the time of Nero, there were sporadic persecutions of Christians by the empire, frequently because religion and politics were closely aligned. Acknowledgement of the official Roman religion often served as a sort of litmus test for patriotism. The stories of those who suffered and died because they refused to deny their heavenly Lord in favor of the earthly lordship of Caesar have been a powerful witness to Christians of every other generation. Even in their own day, their testimony attracted many converts from paganism, so that "the blood of the martyrs was the seed of the church," just as Tertullian had asserted.

Enmity between empire and church was not destined to be a perpetual thing, however, and eventually persecution was to give way to conversion. Indeed, when in 313 A.D. Constantine began the process of making Christianity the official religion of the empire, the church began to encounter an entirely different set of problems. For one thing, large numbers of the uninformed, unconverted, and uncommitted flooded the constituency of the churches—even Constantine himself may have fallen in this category—because of the newly found official sanction. Even the best efforts of the bishops and the theologians could not entirely prevent the persistence of pagan ideas and superstitions in the popular piety of the newly found Christians. Increasing numbers of the truly committed determined to leave behind the chaos of the nominally Christian empire for the shelter and purity of monastic life. To some, at least, it seemed clear that Christianity had lost its soul in gaining imperial favor.

The situation was further complicated, within a century after Constantine, when the venerable Roman Empire collapsed under the increasing pressure of "barbarians" from northern and western Europe. In the aftermath of the debacle, the church was one of the few institutions which survived to preserve and communicate the remains of Roman culture. Literacy came to be virtually unknown outside the monasteries, and even such basic factors as agricultural and medical techniques were remembered primarily by monks and other church workers.

Furthermore, the church had before itself a brand-new missionary challenge. The people who dominated the life of the European continent were no longer representative of stable and sophisticated civilizations such as Greece and Rome. They were products of rather primitive circumstances, and their religious origins had precious little in common with Christianity. Just as Paul had faced the challenge of breaking new ground for the faith in the first century, men such as Columba and the legendary Patrick went out to preach the gospel in areas of Europe which were basically uncharted insofar as the church was concerned. In many ways, the difficulties they encountered paralleled those described for us in the Acts account of Paul's earlier efforts, and the successes they achieved are almost equally remarkable.

The Church in the Middle Ages

The importance of the church as the conservator of western civilization during the thousand years after the fall of the Roman Empire can hardly be overestimated. Not only did its institutions, such as the monasteries, serve as repositories for knowledge and technique; its leaders served to provide guidance and authority for a society which frequently bordered on anarchy. In particular, the bishop of Rome, who by the end of the sixth century was universally acknowledged as the head of western Christendom, was able to exercise great power in the affairs of European life. Pope Gregory I (ca. 540–604 A.D.), for example, served not only as a spiritual father for the church but also as a political and diplomatic leader for the Roman community as well. He stepped into a political vacuum to lead the defense of Rome against Lombard aggression, and developed social services which preserved the lives of the impoverished citizenry of the city.

As the centuries passed, the power of the papacy continued to grow until it reached its zenith under Hildebrand, who became Pope Gregory VII in 1073 A.D. By that time the pope not only claimed to be supreme head of the whole church, but he also claimed temporal powers, including the right to crown and uncrown kings. Gregory VII had sufficient power to humiliate Emperor Henry IV of Germany by forcing him to stand barefoot in the snow at Canossa, seeking papal release from excommunication.

In 1302 Pope Boniface VIII issued an edict expressing the extent of the papal claims to worldly power. Citing the gospel passage in which Jesus acknowledges his disciples' possession of two swords with the statement, "It is enough" (Luke 22:38), Boniface said that the two swords represent spiritual power and temporal power. "Therefore, both are in the power of the church, namely, the spiritual sword and the temporal sword; the latter is to be used for the church, the former by the church; the former by the hand of the priest, the latter by the hand of princes and kings, but at the nod and sufferance of the priest. The one sword must necessarily be subject to the other, and the temporal authority to the spiritual."

This accession of power was attended by growing tendencies toward corruption in the life of the Christian community. Although there were notable exceptions, such as the saintly Franciscan monk who served briefly in 1294 as Pope Celestine V before becoming the only pope ever to abdicate the office, as a rule the later medieval popes were far from admirable. The decline of the papacy was representative of the general state of affairs throughout the Roman church. The popular piety of the laity had become heavily laced with superstition and scrupulosity. Many of the clergy took their standards of commitment and behavior from the unsavory examples set by the popes and their companions. Monastic life, which had begun as a haven for righteousness, had largely degenerated into a way for claiming worldly wealth and pleasures while clinging to the fiction of saintliness. Even the theology of the church had been perverted into a mechanical, tit-for-tat legalism which frequently served self-interest rather than sanctity. In fine, there was ample warrant for improvement in European Christianity as the Middle Ages drew to a close.

Protest and Reform

All through the centuries there had been some individuals and groups within the church who set themselves to the task of purifying or reforming the Christian community. Men like Montanus, Benedict, Francis of Assisi, and Savanarola sought serious renovation of Christianity, and some of them managed to found movements which carried on their efforts after their deaths. Not all of these men and movements were strictly orthodox in their convictions, and not all of their emphases were good. Nevertheless, they shared a conviction that the church needed to be called back to its original standards and ideals.

By and large, though, such efforts did not serve to stem the tide. As the time of the Protestant Reformation approached, the Roman church was probably less amenable to reform than at almost any previous time. The efforts of such men as John Wycliffe in England and Jan Hus in Bohemia were greeted with violent animosity by the religious authorities. When reformation finally came, however, it was the nerve center of a thoroughgoing upheaval which encompassed political, social, and economic aspects of life as well as the spiritual. When on October 31, 1517, Martin Luther nailed his ninety-five theses to the door of the Castle Church in Wittenburg, Germany, he set in motion a reaction against the whole order fostered by medieval Catholicism which was eventually to shake the church to her roots, and lay the basis for reconstruction in all her parts.

Chapter Two

PRESBYTERIANISM
AND THE REFORMATION

The Spread of Protestantism

From the first, Martin Luther's spiritual pilgrimage was an intensely personal thing. Raised a devout Catholic and eventually ordained to the priesthood against parental misgivings, he had been haunted by the problem of human sinfulness. If God is truly righteous, how can he tolerate human sin? Conversely, if man is unrighteous, how can he hope for mercy when he is judged by a sinless God? Medieval Catholicism had devised a variety of ways of answering this question, most of which involved the performance of good works or the payment of fees to the church in order to regain God's favor. Luther had tried hard to be a part of this system. He later commented that if ever a monk had sought salvation by "monkery," he had been that man. In his case, though, all the legalistic devices simply enhanced his frustration.

When he finally found an answer, it came not through improved behavior but through a new understanding of the biblical teaching concerning the grace of God. At some point during his early career as a teacher of theology, while he was doing a painstaking analysis of the book of Psalms and Paul's letters to the Galatians and the Romans, Luther discovered the doctrine which literally saved his life: justification by faith. God's grace, mediated not through human efforts but through his gift of faith, is the only means of our salvation. It was an old truth which had been obscured by centuries of misinterpretation, and it brought Luther back from the brink of despair.

Within a matter of years, this private and personal discovery became a hotly controverted public issue. Luther was the proverbial man groping in the darkness who seizes a bellrope and wakes the whole community. In this instance, indeed, the waking community was all of Europe. Luther's new understanding of what it means to be a Christian posed a direct challenge to the authority of the church of Rome, and, when he was eventually forced to repudiate its teachings in favor of what he understood to be the clear guidance of Scripture, an irrevokable division in western Christianity was the result. Throughout Europe, small clusters of protesters or Protestants announced their fealty to the Bible rather than to the Catholic hierarchy as the final authority in religion, and set out to reorganize the structure and behavior of their communities in line with their newly found commitments.

One particularly fertile ground for the new movement was Switzerland. Shortly after Luther's initial protest, a vigorous leader named Huldrich Zwingli undertook a thoroughgoing revision of religious life in the city of Zurich, and many other Swiss cities were not far behind. In many respects, Zwingli and his colleagues advocated a change even more radical than Luther had envisioned. Whereas Luther simply desired the elimination of all aspects of Catholic belief and practice which were prohibited by Scripture, the Zwinglians required that nothing be done which was not specifically required by the Word of God. This basic approach is the reason for the label "Reformed," which is sometimes given to the churches growing from this particular wing of the Protestant movement.

Zwingli's leadership in Swiss Protestantism was cut short by his death in battle in 1531. Other able men emerged, such as Heinrich Bullinger at Zurich, John Oecolampadius at Basel, and William Farel at Geneva, to nurture the reformation among Swiss Christians. Soon Switzerland became a center for Protestant activity and a sort of staging area for its expansion into other parts of Europe. The one man most responsible for this development, of course, was John Calvin.

The Emergence of John Calvin

John Calvin was born in Noyon, a cathedral town of France fifty miles northeast of Paris, on July 10, 1509. His father, who was a lay official on the bishop's staff, envisioned a career in the church for his bright young son. At the age of fourteen, John entered the University of Paris, where he studied Latin, logic, and philosophy with such self-forgetful diligence that he permanently impaired his health. Later he decided to study law, and spent several years studying at the Universities of Orleans and Bourges under the greatest professors of law who could be found in France. Traces of his legal training seem to appear from time to time in his later theological works.

After his father's death, when he was free to make a choice for himself, Calvin decided to turn from the law to the study of classical literature. His first book, for which he received praise as a budding young scholar, was a commentary on Seneca's *Treatise on Clemency.* Calvin's references to fifty-six Latin and twenty-two Greek authors in the commentary give us some indication of his familiarity with the ancient sources.

Events soon took place in his life, however, which turned his career away from this promising beginning as a humanist scholar. Sometime in late 1533 or early 1534, Calvin was converted to Protestantism. The details of this change are not especially clear. He refers to it in passing as a "sudden conversion," and we can presume from subsequent events that it was as definite as it was sudden. Within a matter of months, his newly found convictions had gotten Calvin into trouble. He was suspected—quite properly—of being the ghost writer for an all-too-Protestant address given by a friend who had been elected rector of the University of Paris, and soon Calvin found it necessary to flee the city for his life.

Much of the next three years was spent in a pillar-to-post existence, travelling under an assumed name, living with friends, and doing some very perceptive thinking and writing about the basis for his commitment to the Protestant movement. In the spring of 1536, he published a thoughtful little book on theology, which he named *The Institutes of the Christian Religion.* The book represented his effort to explain Protestantism in systematic fashion, and Calvin dedicated it to King Francis of France, in an attempt to persuade him to look more favorably upon the new movement. Francis was apparently unconvinced, but the theologians of Protestantism were profoundly impressed. Still well under thirty years of age, Calvin came to be esteemed as a major spokesman for their cause. He continued to revise and enlarge the *Institutes,* so that it eventually filled two large volumes and was translated into practically every language of Europe. From that day to the present, it has served as an important "textbook" of Protestantism.

Calvin Comes to Geneva

The publication of this book probably determined the eventual course of Calvin's life work. His fame preceded him as he travelled in search of a place of relative safety in which he could settle into the quiet life of a scholar. One day in August of 1536, Calvin stopped at an inn in Geneva, Switzerland, en route to Strassburg, where he hoped to find a home. But God had other plans for him.

William Farel, the fiery reformer who had spearheaded the Protestant efforts in Geneva, paid the traveller a most unusual visit. Farel gave Calvin an invitation to stay in Geneva and help in the development of the reformation there. But it was an invitation followed by the warning that to leave Geneva behind in quest of scholarly quietude was to court damnation! Let Calvin tell the story himself: "Then Farel, finding he gained nothing by entreaties, besought God to curse my retirement and the tranquility of my studies if I should withdraw and refuse to give assistance when the necessity was so urgent. By this imprecation I was so struck with terror that I desisted from the journey I had undertaken." Thus a visit of one night was to be expanded into a life's vocation.

He began his work in Geneva on September 1, 1536, by preaching a sermon in St. Peter's Cathedral. A simple, expository sermon on a text from one of Paul's letters, it was the first of hundreds that Calvin was to preach from that pulpit. These sermons, in which Calvin went directly to the Bible for guidance in everything relating to the church and the Christian life, were the basis upon which he began to reform the life of Geneva. He and Farel set to work at once preparing a master plan for the moral and spiritual renovation of the community. They drafted a Confession of Faith, a Catechism, and a Book of Discipline, which were approved by the City Council in July of 1537 and proclaimed to the citizens of Geneva as their new constitution. Some of them decided to dig in their heels against such sweeping changes, and eventually they raised sufficient commotion to force Farel and Calvin from the city in the spring of the following year. Farel settled in Neuchatel and never again returned to Geneva. Calvin went to Strassburg, his original destination before his encounter with Farel in the Geneva inn two years before.

Exile and Return

Strassburg received Calvin with open arms. Martin Bucer, the leader of the reformation there, turned out to be the sort of colleague from whom Calvin could derive theological insight as well as personal support. The expanded edition of the *Institutes* which appeared in 1539 gives evidence of Calvin's growth during this time. There were also many French-speaking Protestant refugees in the city, and Calvin was chosen to organize them into a congregation and serve as their pastor. Borrowing aspects of the typical service of worship conducted by Bucer, he established the simple but moving liturgical pattern which is still used in the worship of many presbyterian churches in our own time.

Calvin's service substituted a sermon and the Lord's Supper for the Roman mass. The communion table was central, and the entire service, with the exception of the reading and exposition of Scripture, was conducted by the minister standing at the table. Calvin balanced set patterns of worship with freedom from forms, and he approved the use of both read and spontaneous prayers. There was hearty congregational singing of Psalms, but no musical instruments, since they were thought to be reminiscent of the worldliness of medieval traditions.

In August of 1540, Calvin married Idelette de Bure, a widow with a teen-age son and a younger daughter. Farel described his friend's bride as "not only good and honorable but also handsome." Calvin's own references to her are few, and some of them appear to be quite condescending to modern eyes. (After her death, he commented that he had "never experienced the slightest hindrance from her"!) Nevertheless, the two seem to have been very happy in their life in the decade between their marriage and Idelette's death.

The newlyweds were not destined to be permanent residents of Strassburg, however, because local affairs at Geneva had gone from bad to worse after the expulsion of Calvin and Farel. The people who had balked at the constitutional codes recommended by the reformers had led the city into a time of political and spiritual peril. The Roman Catholic church, through the efforts of the wise and urbane Cardinal Sadolet, was trying to coax the city back into the fold. The pastors who had replaced Calvin and Farel left the city for greener pastures. All in all, the memory of the two exiles grew ever fonder for Genevan Protestants as time passed.

In the fall of 1540, both were invited by the City Council to return to their previous positions. Farel flatly refused, but Calvin was eventually persuaded to go back. Feeling that God was calling him to complete the job he had begun in Geneva, he returned amidst general rejoicing to resume the task which was to occupy the rest of his life.

Beginning Anew

Calvin took up his work where he had left off at the time of his banishment, and he did so without apology. He gave the City Council two prerequisites for his return. He asked, first of all, for the establishment of a written religious constitution for the city. Secondly, he wanted to be placed in charge of a uniform program of religious instruction for all the inhabitants of the city. Six weeks after his return to Geneva, he submitted to the Council the *Draft Ecclesiastical Ordinances,* a document which was to serve as the basic pattern for religious life in Geneva for the next three centuries. In it, Calvin gave his basic interpretation of the biblical mode of church government and discipline.

His plan of organization provided for a very simple form of representative government for the church. He proposed that church officers be designated as he found them described in the New Testament: elders, pastors, teachers, and deacons. Each of these officers was to be chosen by the community to exercise authority over it in his particular area of responsibility. Calvin's original plan seems to have embodied more religious independence than the city government was willing to allow, so the details were modified somewhat by the city fathers. Nevertheless, for the times it represented a remarkable movement away from political domination of the church.

The key to Calvin's program was the establishment of a disciplinary commission, called the Consistory, which was composed of twelve lay elders and the "venerable company" of local pastors. In some respects, the Consistory was like the session of a modern Presbyterian church; in others, it was somewhat like our modern presbyteries. It had the task of governing the church and administering the personal behavior of the people. Detailed rules for Christian living were drawn up, and it was the

duty of the Consistory to see that people observed them. The records
show that people were disciplined for various offenses, including cursing,
visiting taverns, adultery, playing cards on Sunday, singing dirty songs,
attempting suicide—even arranging a marriage between a woman of
seventy and a man of twenty-five!

"The Most Perfect School of Christ"

Personal behavior was not the only matter of concern to Calvin as
he returned to Geneva; indeed it probably was not even first on his list.
His primary intention was to assure the proper religious instruction of
the inhabitants of the city. If faith became vital and correct, morals
would surely follow. To this end, he saw to it that church attendance
was made compulsory. A steady, systematic exposure to the Word was
essential, and it was Calvin's practice to preach his way through a book
of the Bible, a few verses at a time.

Calvin also received the approval of the City Council for a revised
version of the Confession of Faith and Catechism that he and Farel had
prepared for Geneva before their departure in 1537. These documents,
which have borne the city's name down through the centuries, are
among the clearest statements of what was to be called Calvinist theology; and they were to have marked influence upon confessions and
creeds later to be formulated in France, the Netherlands, Scotland, and
England.

In order to propagate this theology, Calvin began to design a
system of public education for Geneva, beginning with primary schools
and ending with the Academy (or University) where young men might
be prepared for the ministry or other professions. The schools were
controlled by the church and presided over by the clergy, thus providing
a ready and natural means of passing the faith from one generation to
the next.

Geneva quickly gained international esteem as a center for Protestant education. From all over Europe, visitors and refugees came because of Calvin and his brand of Christianity. In the decade following
1549, over five thousand immigrants came to Geneva, which had con-
tained a total of only thirteen thousand residents at the beginning of
that period. Some of the newcomers, especially the French, were fleeing
religious persecution. Geneva was to serve them as a base of operations

as they sought to reform the religious life of their home countries.

No man ever worked harder at a task than did John Calvin. He preached several times each week, taught theology, wrote commentaries, superintended a whole system of schools, wrote books and pamphlets, carried on an extensive correspondence with reformation leaders all over Europe, and maintained oversight of the reform movement in Geneva. Even after his return from exile, however, his course in that city was not altogether smooth. From about 1545 to 1555, a well-organized group of citizens—many of them from the first families of the city—offered vigorous opposition to Calvin's policies. In 1553, this anti-Calvin faction gained the majority in the City Council, and for a time it appeared that the famous reformer might once again be forced to leave his adopted home.

It was while his opponents were in power that Calvin was called to testify against Michael Servetus, the brilliant heretic whose case has often been seen as a *cause célèbre* in the history of religious intolerance. Calvin was clearly offended by the man, and argued for his conviction as a heretic. He was convicted and condemned to die, and after refusing Calvin's plea for a more humane method of execution, the council had him burned at the stake. The whole story of Servetus is a sad one, and Calvin certainly does not appear at his best in it. But we need to bear in mind the pattern set by the century in which he lived—and by our own—before making self-righteous judgments on the case. In 1903 a group of loyal "sons of Calvin" erected a monument as an expression of sorrow for the burning of Servetus. Such repentance has been expressed for few other acts of religious persecution.

Not long after the Servetus affair, Calvin's opponents were completely discredited in the eyes of the citizens of Geneva. Most of them were either arrested or driven from the city in May of 1555, and Calvin once again became preeminent in the affairs of the community. Geneva entered upon a time of unparallelled prosperity. In many ways the spiritual fervor of the citizens seems to have complemented their efforts in more worldly affairs. The commercial activity and social development blended with the moral and spiritual commitments of the citizens. John Knox, who was a refugee there from 1554 to 1559, remarked in retrospect that Geneva had been "the most perfect school of Christ that ever was in the earth since the days of the Apostles."

Our Debt to Calvin

John Calvin died on May 27, 1564, leaving the affairs of his adopted city in the capable hands of Theodore Beza and a number of other "Calvinists" who would seek to emulate the efforts of their teacher.

Even those who are not Calvinist or Presbyterian in their direct heritage find it necessary to acknowledge the tremendous impact of John Calvin upon the subsequent history of western civilization. Leaving aside for the moment his obvious contributions to the development of protestant Christianity, Calvin has been credited—or blamed—for providing the motivation for far-reaching developments in social, economic, and political life. Such diverse institutions as public schools, industrial capitalism, and modern democracy have been seen by many as products of Calvin's approach to life.

It has even been said, with varying degrees of accuracy, that his ideas provide the basic structure for American civilization. The German historian Leopold von Ranke, for example, boldly asserted that "John Calvin was the virtual founder of America." While such broad statements deserve careful qualification, as we shall presently see, the thoughts and actions of this one man have profoundly influenced European and American life.

Chapter Three

PRESBYTERIANISM
ON THE CONTINENT

The Spread of Calvinism

The genius of John Calvin was clearly not foreordained to be the possession of the city of Geneva alone. His ideas on theology and church organization soon gained wide currency throughout European Protestantism. Calvin kept up a voluminous correspondence with people all over Europe, and was quick to offer practical advice for local circumstances or detailed explanations of his theological point of view. "Graduates" of the "perfect school of Christ" had soon made their way to the far corners of the continent. Reformed churches emerged in such places as Germany, Czechoslovakia (then known as Bohemia), Poland, Hungary, and even Italy and Spain. Frequently, as in the latter two cases, the groups were quite small and feeble, but their very existence was testimony to the value of Calvin's system. Geneva had become the mother of a movement.

It would carry us afield from the purpose of this volume to go into the detailed history of all of these groups. We do need to spend some time, however, in reviewing the stories of two of the continental Reformed churches, since they have special bearing upon later developments in North America. Then we shall turn to the development of presbyterianism in Great Britain.

The Rise of Protestantism in France

The beginnings of Protestantism in France date back to the generation before young John Calvin was a student in the French universities.

Some of the scholars in France, impressed by the fresh spirit of Renaissance humanism, began to undertake the careful study of the Bible in its original languages. One of them, a Paris professor named Jacques Lèfevre d'Etaples, produced a French translation of the New Testament in 1523, which was eagerly read by many people. Although Lèfevre and most of his contemporaries never formally left the Roman Catholic church, their work laid the foundation for the conversions of other French Christians, such as Farel and Calvin. At first, even King Francis I and his sister Margaret were somewhat open to the new movement. Margaret's daughter, Jeanne d'Albret, was avowedly a Protestant, and Jeanne's son, Henry of Navarre, was destined to figure significantly in the later fortunes of French Christianity.

As the Protestant ferment in France increased, however, Francis I reaffirmed strong Catholic convictions and began a policy of suppression which was to lead to eventual tragedy in the religious history of France. The flight of Calvin, which was described in the previous chapter, was one among many such stories which could be told of the exodus of French Protestants. Nevertheless, there were others who chose the insecure alternative of remaining both Protestant and residents of France at the same time. Although they were in rather constant peril, their movement developed into a warm and vital Christian community.

The story of the founding of the first Protestant congregation in France typifies the gentle piety of these Christians. In 1555 a new baby was born into a Protestant family in Paris. At that time, the Protestants were still gathering informally in private homes for worship and study, without any ordained pastoral leadership. The parents of the child wanted it baptized by a Protestant minister, but there was none nearer than Geneva, which was more than three hundred miles away. The friends of the family determined to organize a church and elect a pastor, so that the young Protestant could have a proper reception into the Body of Christ.

This event was a spark for the organization of other congregations. As though by chain reaction, over the next six years nearly two thousand congregations with a presbyterian form of government and a Calvinistic system of doctrine had been organized in France. Many of the churches were supplied by ministers trained by Calvin in Geneva, and dispatched secretly across the border into France. All told, Geneva sent at least 120 of these undercover "missionaries" into France in the next seventeen years, and there may have been many others whose identity went undiscovered.

In May of 1559, French Protestants organized themselves into a nationwide presbyterian system, which included consistories (sessions), colloquies (presbyteries), provincial synods, and a national synod. A Reformed confession of faith, worked out with the consultation and advice of Calvin, was adopted. People of all classes of French society were attracted to the newly organized church, which began to be called by the name *Huguenot.*

Religious Wars in France

The emergence of the Huguenots as a national church was a matter of grave concern to both Catholic and royal authorities in France, and there seems to have been little hesitation to resort to military force to subdue the movement. The Protestants, however, had some notable political and military leaders on their side as well, such as Admiral Coligny, Prince Henry of Navarre, and the Duke of Condé. They began to organize for self defense. Calvin strongly advised against any show of force that might be interpreted as conspiracy or armed resistance. In words that were to be sadly prophetic, he wrote, "If one drop of blood is shed in such a revolt, rivers will flow; it is better that we all perish than to cause such a scandal to the cause of Christ and His evangel."

Without tracing the political intricacies of the times, we must nevertheless tell the sad outcome of this growing animosity between Protestants and Catholics in France. Eventually blood was shed, and, as Calvin had predicted, the conflict issued into a series of so-called "wars of religion" which were to be a blight on the life of the French nation for more than a century. Many thousands of Christians on both sides of the controversy were to lose their lives, and thousands more were forced to leave their homeland in order to find peace.

In the midst of the conflict, one of the most horrible atrocities in Christian history took place. In August of 1572, thousands of Protestants had come to Paris for the marriage of Prince Henry, the Protestant ruler of Navarre, to the Catholic princess, Marguerite de' Medici. Many viewed the marriage as a possible bridge between the two warring factions in France. Behind the scenes, however, a conspiracy had been laid to kill all of the Protestants in the city. Just before dawn on St. Bartholomew's Day (August 24), at the ringing of the bell of the Cathedral of St. Germain, the slaughter was begun. Most of the Protestant leaders, including Admiral Coligny, were murdered, and the shock waves of the Paris massacre evoked echoes of similar violence throughout the nation. It is estimated that somewhere between 30,000 to 70,000 Huguenots were slain in France during the next six weeks, and the Protestant cause there never really recovered from the blow.

In 1589 the harried Protestants gained a brief respite from persecution when Henry of Navarre became King Henry IV of France. Although he had been forced to convert to Catholicism in order to become king, Henry did not forsake the Protestant cause. In 1598 he issued the famous Edict of Nantes, which gave religious toleration to the Huguenots. After his assassination in 1610, however, persecution was resumed, and Protestants were once again deprived of their religious and civil rights. Eventually, in 1685, Louis XIV revoked the long-ignored edict of toleration, and for a period thereafter systematic legal prosecution of Huguenots was again the order of the day.

The Huguenot Legacy

During all this time of suffering, thousands of French Protestants fled their homeland. Many of them eventually found their way into the British colonies of North America. Of those who came, only a few were concerned to maintain their national identity. Because of their bitter memories, most Huguenots quickly left behind the French language and culture, and joined themselves to English-speaking churches—frequently Presbyterian congregations of English and Scottish background.

Despite the bloody heritage, which earned for it the designation "the Church of the Cross," French Protestantism has survived to the present day. At last reckoning, there were in excess of 375,000 members and adherents of the Reformed Church of France. From its seminary at the University of Montpelier, clergymen go out to represent the Calvinist heritage throughout the French-speaking world. The influence of the Huguenots and their descendents has always been far more significant than the actual numbers involved in the movement. As one French pastor of the nineteenth century summed up its legacy, "I represent a great Presbyterian Church; I may say the greatest when I think of what she has suffered for the cause of Christ and human liberty. And though we are small now, we may say that our poverty has been the riches of many nations."

The Rise of Protestantism in the Netherlands

The Netherlands also proved to be fertile ground for Protestantism. Even before the teachings of Luther made their way into Belgium and Holland, the renewal of Catholic piety which was called "modern devotion" had been fostered there by the movement known as the Brothers of the Common Life. When the Reformation came, there was a response from many who had been yearning for a new expression of faith. Luther's teachings had early currency, but Calvinism made a deeper and more permanent impression. It was a number of years before the Protestant movement in the Netherlands was organized into a church, but sentiment spread rapidly nonetheless. As early as 1531 there were twenty-five translations of the Bible into the various vernaculars of the Low Countries.

It was not until 1561, though, that the movement began to crystallize into an organized church. In that year, Guy de Brès, a minister who had been educated under Calvin at Geneva, drafted a confession for Low Country Protestants which came to be known as the Belgic Confession. In 1563 a presbyterian constitution was drafted by a conference in Antwerp, and congregations began to be organized around the countryside. Eight years later a synod was organized, modelled on the basic plan of the Reformed Church of France. One unusual feature of the system established for the Netherlands was the fact that no matter how many congregations there might be in a city, they were all to be governed by one session. This is known as the collegiate church system.

Conflict and Persecution

Sad to say, opposition to Protestantism was also constant and severe, even from the earliest stirrings. Luther's writings were condemned almost as soon as they arrived, and in July of 1523 two Augustinian monks were burned in Brussels by Catholic authorities for holding Protestant beliefs. These were portents of greater difficulties to follow.

The tension was heightened by the fact that the religious controversy came to be an aspect of the struggle for political independence in the Netherlands. Spain, which controlled the region at the outbreak of the Reformation, was staunchly Roman Catholic and intended that all of its domain should remain so. On the other side, the native prince, William of Orange—popularly misnamed William the Silent—encouraged the Protestant cause and associated its hopes with his own ambition to have freedom from Spain. In 1573 he actually became a Protestant, and derived substantial military support from his new coreligionists against the hated Duke of Alva. Under William's leadership, the seven northern provinces of the Netherlands eventually won their independence, and the Dutch Republic was established in 1579. This is how it came to pass that Holland has a large Protestant population to this day, while Belgium, the former southern provinces, is still predominantly Roman Catholic.

Theological Ferment in Holland

Among other things, the victory of William's forces and the consequent dominance of Reformed Protestantism in Holland fostered the establishment of a system of great universities, which were to serve as centers of theological activity on the continent. The University of Leyden, for example, which was established as William's reward to the citizens of that community for their stalwart resistance to a Spanish siege, became a focal point for the teaching of Calvinist theology on the continent. Some Dutch theologians, such as Francis Gomarus, even out-Calvined Calvin himself in their zeal on certain key points of doctrine. This precipitated a great theological controversy which was to continue for a good many years.

The controversy came to a head when another Leyden professor, whose theological name was Jacobus Arminius, protested against the hyper-Calvinism of some of his colleagues. Arminius was concerned to emphasize the reality of human decision and activity in the Christian life over against his opponents' somewhat mechanical view of the arbitrary dominance of God. Arminius died while the debate was still developing, but the Arminian or Remonstrant cause was carried on by his supporters. The controversy reached such a pitch that finally the government decided to call a council of theologians to settle the matter once and for all. The council, known as the Synod of Dort, was convened in November of 1618, and continued its sessions until the following May.

Over a hundred delegates participated, almost half of whom had come from outside Holland. James I of England sent a number of delegates from the Anglican Church, with instructions "to mitigate the heat on both sides, and to advise the Dutch ministers not to deliver in the pulpit to the people those things for ordinary doctrines which are the highest points of schools and not fit for vulgar capacity, but disputable on both sides." That was probably good advice for subsequent generations as well!

The "Five Points"

The discussions at Dort centered primarily on five aspects of Christian doctrine which have come to be known, somewhat inaccurately, as the "Five Points of Calvinism." In actuality, they are simply five doctrines which the Arminians disputed and the Calvinists defended. They do not include many essential aspects of Calvin's doctrinal system, such as the emphasis on the absolute sovereignty of God, which is a sort of central sun around which all the other doctrines should revolve.

A helpful method for remembering the "Five Points," time-honored by the usage of generations of catechumens and seminary students, is an acrostic on the word "TULIP." The points are as follows:

> Total depravity;
> Unconditional election;
> Limited atonement;
> Irresistible grace;
> Perseverance of the saints.

Let us consider each in turn:

"Total depravity" does not mean that the unregenerate person is as wicked as he or she can possibly be—though some appear to strive mightily in the endeavor—but that every aspect of his nature is distorted or tainted by evil, so that there can be no conceivable way of self-salvation.

"Unconditional election" means that God's choice of a person for everlasting life is in no way determined by some foreknowledge of the person's faith or good behavior or anything of that kind. God chooses, as a later confessional statement puts it, "out of his mere good pleasure," for reasons which have not been revealed to us.

"Limited atonement" means that Christ's reconciling act, though *adequate* for all humankind, is *beneficial* only for the elect. Those who have not been chosen by God may be edified by the example of Christ, but they will not be saved by his work.

"Irresistible grace" means that when God undertakes to save a person by his grace or unmerited favor, that grace is invincible. Even in making every effort, a person could not refuse it. Therefore no credit should be due for accepting it.

"Perseverance of the saints," which might perhaps be more accurately described as "perseverance of God's Spirit," is the affirmation that once God has chosen, regenerated and adopted a sinner into his family, there is no power strong enough to extract that "saint" from his care.

The Legacy of Dutch Calvinism

Ultimately, the Synod of Dort decided to condemn the Arminian views, which ran contrary to these five affirmations. Sadly, we must confess that again our forebears took part in acts of religious persecution, for those who advocated the Arminian position were deposed and banished from Holland. It must be said, however, that the final decisions of the synod did not constitute a reversion to hyper-Calvinism, as some have insisted, but an attempt to state a mainstream point of view for those standing in the Reformed tradition. The confession formulated at Dort, which is called "The Canons of the Synod of Dort," has been a part of the constitution of the Dutch Reformed Church right down to modern times.

Three and a half centuries have passed since the Arminian controversy, and some would say that Dutch Protestantism still exhibits the same sorts of tensions which evoked controversy in that former day. Nevertheless, this resolutely Calvinistic flavor has permeated the cultural development of the entire nation. Today over four million residents of the Netherlands are members of Reformed churches.

Dutch colonists in the new world continued the same theological tradition here. The Dutch Reformed church continued to prosper in New York even after the British takeover there, and the heritage continues today, not only in our American Presbyterian churches, but in the Reformed Church in America and the Christian Reformed Church.

Chapter Four

PRESBYTERIANISM
IN SCOTLAND

Scottish Christianity

The richness of our heritage is certainly well exemplified by the contributions of the French and Dutch Protestants who had to suffer for the privilege of passing the tradition to their descendents. It is not too much to say, however, that the contributions of another group of Reformed Christians exerted more direct influence on American Presbyterianism than all the continental churches combined. That group, of course, is the Scottish church.

The history of Christianity in Scotland reaches back to a heroic missionary named Columba, who came in 563 A.D. to the island of Iona, off the west coast of Scotland, where he established a Christian center (reconstructed in recent years) from which he undertook the evangelization of the mainland. Scottish Christianity in those early days enjoyed a certain measure of independence from the affairs of the Roman Catholic church. Some have even made the claim—probably exaggerated—that the early monastic system in Scotland was technically presbyterian in polity. At any rate, it was different for awhile; but when Celtic Christianity became part and parcel of the Roman system, even the shortcomings of medieval Catholicism were zealously incorporated into the native piety. In few instances was the state of churchly affairs any lower than in Scotland at the eve of the Reformation. Scottish religion was notorious for its ignorance, superstition, and wickedness in high places.

Origins of the Scottish Reformation

When the Reformation came to Scotland, it was greeted with the same sort of hostility which typified the continental experiences already noted. Patrick Hamilton, a young nobleman who taught at St. Andrews University, might be called the morning star of the Scottish Reformation. Hamilton had converted to Lutheranism while studying on the continent, and upon his return he began to teach and preach his new faith, despite a legal ban against all forms of Protestantism. He fled the country once, but soon returned to resume his advocacy of the Lutheran cause. His family name protected him only briefly; the Archbishop of St. Andrews had him arrested and burned at the stake on February 28, 1528.

Hamilton's death, however, was not the death of the spirit of Protestantism in Scotland. One interpreter informed the archbishop that the smoke of the immolation of "Maister Patrick" had infected everybody it touched. Among those who emerged in the leadership of the Protestant cause was a notable scholar named George Wishart, who had been teaching at Cambridge before removing to Scotland. We are told that Wishart was accompanied in his travels through Scotland by a young priest-turned-Protestant named John Knox, whose job it was to stand with drawn sword to keep back the mob. Knox was later to prove his mettle in verbal combat under conditions that would make swordplay seem easier, if not preferable, by comparison.

Wishart, like Hamilton, was a target for Catholic persecution. He was eventually arrested, tried for heresy, and burned at the stake under orders from Cardinal David Beaton in March of 1546. A few weeks later, some of Wishart's supporters sought revenge for his death. They forced their way into St. Andrews Castle, murdered Cardinal Beaton, and hung his dead body from the castle wall as a public insult to the Catholics. Protestant leaders, fearing the inevitable reprisals, fled to the castle and barricaded themselves there for protection.

Knox as a Reformer

Among those in the castle was John Knox, who was soon chosen by the rebels to serve as their preacher. His first "parish," however, was soon brutally dissolved. When the Scottish Catholics were unable to regain the castle, they sent for French soldiers who were quartered in Scotland, and the French used their artillery to batter their way in. Knox and his comrades were taken into custody, and for the next year and a half he was a slave on a French galley ship which plied the waters between Scotland and France. According to his later account, the physical hardships he had to endure were greatly aggravated by the daily repetition of Catholic rituals by the French crew.

Eventually his release was obtained through the good offices of English authorities, and Knox found a temporary home in exile there. He was chosen to be one of the court preachers for young King Edward VI, whose Protestant sympathies made England a haven for such men as Knox. When Edward died shortly thereafter, however, he was succeeded by his Catholic half-sister, the notorious "Bloody Mary," who instituted a vigorous campaign to bring her nation back into the Catholic camp.

Knox joined numerous other "Marian exiles" in fleeing to the continent in order to avoid the sort of fate which had earlier befallen Hamilton and Wishart. He spent three years in Geneva with John Calvin, who was then at the height of his influence. The French Knox had learned perforce as a galley slave served him in good stead as he learned Calvinism firsthand. Knox also organized the English-speaking refugees in Geneva into a church and became their pastor. A possible index of their aspirations to be done with exile is the fact that this church elected its pastor, elders, and deacons for only one year at a time.

In 1559 Knox's desire to return to Scotland was fulfilled, and he had soon revived the Reformation and laid the groundwork for the establishment of a presbyterian form of church government there. During the early days of this monumental effort, he is said to have prayed, "O God, give me Scotland or I die!" The answer to his prayer came in the drama which unfolded over the remaining years of his life. In August of 1560, the Scottish parliament, persuaded by Knox, officially renounced Roman Catholicism and adopted the Reformed faith for Scotland. John Knox and five other men—all also named John—were directed to prepare a confession of faith for the nation. It took them only four days to lay before the parliament the document which was to be known to later generations as the Scots Confession of 1560, an essential milestone in the theological tradition of the Church of Scotland.

In December of the same year, the first General Assembly of the Scottish church was organized under the leadership of Knox. There were only six ministers and thirty-six ruling elders present, and there were probably fewer than a dozen Protestant ministers in all of Scotland at that time. The assembly spent a large part of its time preparing a Book of Discipline for the church. It provided for a typical presbyterian system of government with pastors, elders, and deacons, except that the elders and deacons were to be elected for only one year at a time, "lest by long continuance of such officers men presume upon the liberty of the church."

In the best Calvinistic tradition, the book also dealt with the manners and morals of the people. Its affirmation of the requirements of Christian ethical activity is a classic of succinctness and clarity: "To save the lives of innocents, to repress tyrannies, to defend the oppressed, to keep our bodies clean and holy, to live in soberness and temperance, to deal justly with all men both in word and deed, and to repress all appetite of our neighbor's hurt, are the good works of the Second Table [of the Decalogue], which are most pleasing and acceptable to God."

Provision was also made in the book for the support of education in a Christian context. Every church was to have a schoolmaster, able to teach Latin, grammar, and the catechism. High schools were provided for, and as a capstone of the academic system there were three—later four—universities, each one of which would have the capacity to train men for the ministry.

Knox and Mary, Queen of Scots

Just as this reformation was well under way in Scotland, Mary Stuart arrived from France to assume her throne as queen of Scotland. Sent to France in infancy by her mother in order to be raised in a Roman Catholic atmosphere, Mary had been married to King Francis II of France in 1558. When Francis died two years later, the eighteen-year-old queen had decided to return to Scotland. Mary ranks as one of the most fascinating and enigmatic rulers of Western history. An ardent Catholic, she was scarcely settled in Holyrood Palace before she had a mass celebrated, even though it was contrary to the law of the land.

John Knox promptly declared from his pulpit that one mass inspired him with more fear than would the landing of an invading army of ten thousand soldiers. Mary heard of the sermon, and summoned the preacher to the palace to give an account of himself. Thus began a verbal duel between the two which had as its prize the religious allegiance of the Scottish nation. In a series of five interviews, neither Knox nor Mary could win. Knox had the capacity to reduce the queen to tears, but she was a tough opponent nonetheless. At times it looked as though she was going to be able to swing Scotland back to Catholicism. Eventually, though, her own folly and misdeeds brought her downfall, and she was forced to abdicate and leave the country. The rest of her sad story—her flight to England, her imprisonment by Queen Elizabeth, and her execution in the Tower of London—is familiar history. With her departure, Protestantism was firmly established in the nation. The prayer of Knox was realized, at least for the time being, before his death in 1572.

Further Struggles

When Knox died, the leadership of the Scottish church fell to Andrew Melville, a scholarly man who had also learned his Calvinism firsthand at Geneva. Among other things, Melville wrought a transformation in the university system in Scotland, serving in turn as principal administrative officer of the universities of Glasgow, Aberdeen, and St. Andrews. Under his leadership, the Church of Scotland also made remarkable progress as an institution. He revised the first Book of Discipline so that a more systematic form of presbyterianism was established.

Melville had many bitter struggles with young James VI, king of Scotland, who in 1603 became James I of England, combining the monarchy of the two nations under one ruler. James had been only an infant when his mother, Mary Stuart, had abdicated. The Scottish reformers had taken charge of his education, in the hope that they would have a Presbyterian king when he reached his majority. They were to be grievously disappointed. James fought the Presbyterians in Scotland (and the Puritans in England) every step of the way, and he was determined to put bishops beholden to him in charge of the Church of Scotland. Andrew Melville, of course, was equally determined that he should not.

Referring to James to his face as "God's silly vassal"—the word then meant "weak" rather than "foolish"—Melville is said to have seized the king by the sleeve of his robe and told him, "Sir, as divers times before I have told you, so now again I must tell you, there are two kings and two kingdoms in Scotland: there is King James, the head of the Commonwealth, and there is Christ Jesus, the King of the Church, whose subject James is, and of whose kingdom he is not a king, nor a lord, nor a head, but a member. We will yield to you in your place, and give you all due obedience, but again I say that you are not the head of the Church."

It should be no surprise that, when James became king of the united monarchy, he locked Melville up in the Tower of London for four years and then banished him from the country. Melville spent his latter years teaching in a Protestant seminary at Sedan in France.

When James died in 1625, his son Charles I became king of England and Scotland. As we shall have occasion to see in greater detail in the next chapter, Charles was even more determined than his father to force the Scottish Presbyterians and their theological cousins, the English Puritans, to conform to the Anglican system of government and worship. He was ably assisted by William Laud, his very aggressive Archbishop of Canterbury. James I had already succeeded in forcing an episcopal structure of sorts upon the recalcitrant Scots, though he had taken great care to leave their local parish organization of elders and ministers intact. Now Charles and Laud determined to force the Anglican form of worship upon them as well.

Charles commanded that on July 23, 1637, every church in Scotland would begin to use the Anglican service. On that day, the Dean of Edinburgh undertook to conduct the services in St. Giles, John Knox's old church, according to Archbishop Laud's prayer book. The popular legend states that he had scarcely begun when a Scottish working woman named Jenny Geddes let out a shout and hurled the stool on which she had been sitting at the dean's head. Whether the legendary Jenny led the way or not, a riotous rebellion broke out that day, not only in St. Giles but all over Scotland, fostered by staunch Presbyterians who would not accede to the Anglican way of worship.

The Scots knew that they would be forced to give an account of themselves for the uproar of that day. They therefore bound themselves together in a National Covenant, in which they agreed to stand by each other and their Presbyterian way of worship even unto death. The movement spread so widely that soon practically every citizen of the nation had affixed his signature to the agreement. The next year, the

General Assembly voted to purge the church of every vestige of Anglicanism, and to restore the Church of Scotland to a thoroughly Presbyterian way.

While this was going on, Charles was preparing his army to invade
Scotland for the purpose of subduing the heroic Presbyterians. The
Scots were equally busy, preparing an army to resist the king. When
Charles saw the extent of the Scottish preparation, he decided that he
did not have the men and money to carry on the war against them, so
he called a meeting of the English parliament in order to requisition the
necessary resources. Soon, of course, he was at war with his own parliament, in what has come to be known as the English Civil War. Eventually, the parliamentary forces, under the leadership of Oliver Cromwell,
defeated the Royalists and Charles was beheaded in January, 1649. The
Commonwealth was established with Cromwell at its head, and England
and Scotland had no king for the next eleven years.

The death of Charles was something of a scandal among the Scots.
Although they had resisted his commands in the sphere of religion, he
had been a Stuart—one of their own, so to speak—and they had not
wanted to see him killed. Thus, after Cromwell's death, the Scots participated in the movement to bring Charles' son back from exile in
Holland. They required him to sign the National Covenant, and then
crowned him King Charles II. It was a bad day's work for the Scots.
Almost at once he reneged his commitment, asserting that "Presbyterianism is no religion for a gentleman." He and his supporters then
enacted the most drastic laws against those who did not conform to
Anglicanism that England and Scotland had ever known.

Once again the Scots bound themselves together by a National
Covenant. The sufferings of the Covenanters, as these adherents came
to be called, were both widespread and severe. This was the infamous
"killing time," in which men, women, and children who espoused the
Presbyterian cause were hunted and tortured. One of the most impressive sights in contemporary Edinburgh is the monument in Greyfriars
churchyard, dedicated to the memory of the Covenanters who were
martyred during the reign of Charles II.

External Toleration; Internal Divisions

Charles died in 1685, and his brother, James II, ruled only briefly
before being driven from the throne by the so-called "Glorious Revolu-

tion" of 1688. He was replaced by his daughter Mary, and her husband, William, the Dutch prince who was a direct descendent of William the Silent. Soon after the arrival of William and Mary, parliament passed a Toleration Act, which ended the persecution of those outside the Church of England. The "killing time" was over, and the prospects for a Presbyterian Scotland brightened considerably.

In 1712, however, another act was passed by the united parliament of England and Scotland which complicated those prospects. This measure was called the Lay Patronage Act, and it served to give the power of appointment of pastors into the hands of a few large property holders. This was a blow at representative, presbyterian government, and it became the source of many divisions in the Scottish church for more than a century afterward.

The first serious secession from the Church of Scotland was led by Ebenezer Erskine in 1733. In his protest against the Lay Patronage Act, Erskine cried: "What difference does a piece of land make between man and man in the affairs of Christ's kingdom? By this act we show respect to the man with the gold ring and the gay clothing, beyond the man with vile raiment and poor attire." Erskine and several other ministers formed the Associate Presbytery, which was destined to subdivide into several small groups in the course of the next century. This Associate Presbytery in Scotland was the direct ancestor of the Associate Reformed Presbyterian Church in America.

In 1752 Thomas Gillespie led another group out of the Church of Scotland, again in reaction to the Lay Patronage Act, and organized a separate Presbyterian body which came to be known as the Relief Synod. In 1843 Thomas Chalmers led yet another group out of the church for much the same reason, and organized the Free Church of Scotland. In this division, which was called "the Great Disruption," almost five hundred Scottish pastors left behind their churches, manses, and salaries in order to strike a blow for the fundamental Presbyterian principle of representative self-government. The Free Church grew into a great church of nearly a half million members. It was a considerable shock for the Church of Scotland to lose this and the several other dissenting movements. Finally in 1874 the Lay Patronage Act was repealed, and the national church has had greater control of its own affairs since that time. The subsequent history has been largely a story of reunion.

Although some have resisted this impulse—the famous "Wee Free" church, for example—reunion has been a dominant feature in Scottish Presbyterianism in the twentieth century. In 1900 the Free Church of Scotland joined the United Presbyterian Church, itself a merger of the Relief Synod with other smaller groups, to form the United Free Church of Scotland. In 1929, the United Free Church rejoined the Church of Scotland, an act which brought the great majority of Scottish Presbyterians into one denomination, which now numbers well over a million communicant members.

The Scottish Legacy

Scottish Presbyterianism might well be called the mother of churches. The Presbyterian Church in Ireland, several branches of the Presbyterian Church in the United States, the Presbyterian Church in Canada, the Presbyterian Church in Australia, and many Presbyterian Churches in the emerging nations can trace their ancestry to the Church of Scotland. Thus the heritage of John Calvin, communicated to the Scots through John Knox, has now spread throughout the world.

Chapter Five

PRESBYTERIANISM
IN ENGLAND

England and the Reformation

When the Protestant Reformation began on the continent, English Christianity gave every appearance of stability within the Roman Catholic camp. Certainly there had been several previous brushfires of innovation, such as the activities of the Lollards and John Wycliffe in the latter fourteenth century. But England at the time of Luther was presided over by Henry VIII, a man whose apparent commitment to Catholicism had earned him the title of Defender of the Faith from a grateful Pope.

Nevertheless, as we know from the oft-told story, Henry was destined to make the break from Rome on the basis of politics (and pulchritude?) without serious reference to the sorts of issues which brought the Reformation to the various other places mentioned in our narrative thus far. In 1534, in the midst of his quest for a male heir to secure the Tudor dynasty, Henry engineered the passage of the Act of Supremacy, by which the king was made the head of the church in England. During his lifetime, the most obvious change in the religious life of his domain was that the property and administrative power of the church now belonged ultimately to the king himself. In the areas of doctrine and worship, however, little change was immediately evident. In short, the English "reformation" was far different from the sorts of things that had taken place in Geneva and in Germany.

At the death of Henry in 1547, his nine-year-old son, Edward VI, became king and head of the church. Edward was frail but intelligent, and he seems to have had a strong personal commitment to the Protestant cause. Under the leadership of his Archbishop of Canterbury, Thomas Cranmer, the Forty-two Articles of Religion (later reduced to thirty-nine) were prepared as a new creed for the English church, and the Book of Common Prayer was published as a means of establishing uniformity of worship in the English congregations. In both of these documents, some of the elements of Calvinist theology are evident, though it is perhaps too much to refer to them as standing directly in the Reformed tradition. A number of additional reforms were effected during Edward's tenure, and it began to look as though England might have a *religious* reformation along the lines of the continental experience after all. But the untimely death of the young king in 1553 brought the element of reactionary sentiment into the story.

As we have seen in the previous chapter, Mary Tudor, known in later history as "Bloody Mary," succeeded to the English throne. She was Edward's half-sister through Henry's first marriage to Catherine of Aragon, fervently Catholic both by upbringing and conviction. Mary at once tried to undo all that her father and half-brother had done in the area of religion, in an attempt to bring England back into the Roman Catholic fold. Archbishop Cranmer and about three hundred others were burned at the stake. Hundreds of other Protestants fled England seeking refuge from Mary's fury. Many of them eventually found their way to Geneva, and joined Knox in the establishment of the English-speaking congregation there. Thus they also had the opportunity to learn a great deal about the Calvinist or Reformed pattern of faith and life firsthand. While in Geneva, some of the refugees under the leadership of William Whittingham and Miles Coverdale made an English translation of the Bible. It became known as the Genevan Version and had a wide circulation in England until it was superceded by the King James Translation. It was among the first small-sized Bibles ever published, and it was the first English version in which the books were divided into chapters and verses.

The Rise of the Puritans

Upon the death of Mary in 1558, Queen Elizabeth came to the throne and had a long and effective reign, extending to 1603. The Act of Supremacy was reinstituted, making Elizabeth the head of the church as her father and half-brother had been before the Marian interlude. Elizabeth allowed the Protestant exiles to return from Geneva and the other havens of refuge on the continent.

Many of them came with the conviction that the Reformation in England had never really been completed. As they resettled in their native land, they began to insist that the Church of England needed to have a purer form of church government, purer doctrines, a purer form of worship, and purer standards of morality. Of course, as a result of this zeal for purity, they were nicknamed "Puritans." This is a term which evokes a very negative image in our day, because of its association with a sour and rigid outlook on life. Puritans have been accused by later critics, for example, of outlawing the sport of bearbaiting in England, not because it gave so much pain to the bear, but because it gave such pleasure to the observers.

As a matter of fact, the original Puritans were not nearly as unattractive as our latter-day caricatures suppose. Basically they were a people who perceived clearly the power of God's transforming love in their own lives, and were determined to discipline themselves—and the whole society in which they lived—in grateful response to that love. In many respects, their lifestyle embodies the effort to carry the implications of the gospel into secular life in a way that few other generations or groups of Christians have done. "Puritans," Alan Simpson has written, "were elect spirits, segregated from the mass of mankind by an experience of conversion, fired by the sense that God was using them to revolutionize human history, and committed to the execution of his Will." As we shall see, their legacies to subsequent English and American history are numerous and pervasive.

They were not popular with Queen Elizabeth, however. She became increasingly alarmed at the growth of their movement, because of their obvious tendency toward independence from state control. She made a vigorous effort to force the Puritans to settle down and conform to the government and worship of the Church of England, and she did manage in the main to keep them in line with her policies. All the while, though, they were establishing strongholds for themselves in the English universities, and publishing innumerable books and pamphlets which propagated their point of view.

The Early Stuarts and the Puritans

As we have already seen, upon the death of Queen Elizabeth in 1603, James VI of Scotland, the son of Mary Stuart, became James I, king of England and Scotland, and head of the church. The Puritans entertained the hope that the new king, who had been educated by the Presbyterians in Scotland, would be their friend and supporter in their efforts to purify the church. As early as the Hampton Court Conference in January of 1604, however, it became clear that their hope was in vain. James had clearly endured too much of the Presbyterian spirit of independence in Scotland. With respect to the Puritans in his new realm, he resolved: "I will make them conform or harry them out of the land or worse."

He did fulfill his vow to some extent. Some Puritans were harried out of the land, such as the colonists who established Plymouth Plantation on the rocky shores of New England in 1620. By and large, though, James was never really successful in his efforts to make the Puritans who stayed in England conform to his demands. Indeed, they were far stronger at the time of his death than they had been at the beginning of his reign.

James was succeeded by his son, Charles I, who reigned from 1625 to 1649. Charles and his chief advisor, Archbishop Laud, were obsessed with the idea of forcing English Puritans and Scottish Presbyterians into conformity with the government and worship of the Anglican church. The Scots, as we have seen, committed themselves to a National Covenant, and gathered an army which was more than a match for the forces Charles had initially dispatched to whip them into line.

The need for more men and money forced Charles into a crucial disadvantage. He had been ruling for several years without the aid of a parliament. Now circumstances compelled the election of a parliament in order to provide the necessary resources for the war against Scotland. To Charles' great dismay, the people elected a Puritan parliament. He speedily dissolved it, and called for another election. The new parliament had a larger majority of Puritans than the first. Charles again ordered the dissolution of the antagonistic body, but this time parliament refused to be disbanded. Charles raised an army of royalist partisans in order to force parliament into submission, but parliament also raised a partisan army in order to defend itself. Thus England found itself in the throes of a civil war, which was to occupy the greatest energies of the nation for the next two decades.

The Westminster Assembly

Among other things, this self-constituted Puritan parliament turned its attention to religious affairs. For seventy-five years Puritans had been insisting that the reformation of the Church of England needed to be prosecuted to its logical conclusion. The time had finally come. Parliament accordingly convened what is known in history as "The Westminster Assembly of Divines." The Assembly was composed of 121 of the ablest Puritan ministers who could be found in England, plus 20 members of the House of Commons and 10 members of the House of Lords. All but two of the ministers had received their ordination at the hands of bishops of the Church of England. Practically all of them were staunchly Calvinist in their theological orientation, since most of them were products of the English universities and their staunchly Puritan training.

On the question of church government, though, there was a genuine variety of opinion within the Assembly. The majority believed in the presbyterian form, as exemplified to them by the Church of Scotland. There were several others, however, who advocated the "independent" or congregational form, and there were even a few who still adhered to the vision of a purified episcopal order for the English church. Some of the longest and warmest debates in the Assembly were over the matter of church government, and the results of the body's work were more tentative in that area than in any other.

The Assembly was first convened at Westminster Abbey in London on July 1, 1643. The beleaguered Charles issued a warning to the participants that their action was tantamount to treason, but they were confirmed in their intentions to begin. The convocation continued in active session for five years, six months, and twenty-two days. During that time there were 1,163 meetings of the full Assembly, and hundreds of meetings of various committees and subcommittees.

Scottish Influence at the Assembly

The Assembly had not been in session for very long before the tide of war began to turn against the parliamentary forces. Parliament hurriedly sent a deputation to Scotland to seek military aid. The Scots agreed to send help on the condition that all members of the Westminster Assembly and all members of parliament sign a "Solemn League and Covenant" to be drawn up by the Scots. The English agreed, thus pledging themselves to join the Scots in the maintenance and defense of the Church of Scotland, and to dedicate themselves to effect a reformation of the church in "England and Ireland, in doctrine, government, worship and discipline, according to the Word of God, and the example of the best reformed churches."

It was further agreed by the English that the Church of Scotland would be allowed to appoint some commissioners to the Westminster Assembly. Six men were sent: four ministers and two ruling elders. These Scottish commissioners took part in the deliberations of the Assembly, but did not vote. Nevertheless, they exercised an influence upon the Assembly out of all proportion to their numbers.

With their arrival and the signing of the Solemn League and Covenant in September, 1643, the Assembly made a radical change of course in its work. Prior to that time the participants had spent most of their time trying to revise the Thirty-nine Articles of the Church of England, and seemed to have no thought of developing a new confession of faith. Now they laid aside the Thirty-nine Articles and proceeded to reform the Church of England root and branch.

The Work of the Westminster Assembly

The Westminster Assembly was devout as well as scholarly. Much time was spent in prayer, and everything was done in a spirit of reverence. Robert Baillie, the Scottish commissioner whose chronicles of the Assembly bring the scenes to life before the eyes of his readers, has given us a description of one of the days which the gathering spent in fasting and prayer. He writes: "After Dr. Twisse had begun with a brief prayer, Mr. Marshall prayed large for two hours, most divinely confessing the sins of the members of the Assembly in a wonderfully pathetic and prudent way. After that, Mr. Arrowsmith preached one hour; then a psalm; thereafter Mr. Vines prayed near two hours, and Mr. Palmer preached one hour, and Mr. Seaman prayed near two hours; then a psalm. After that Mr. Henderson brought them to a short, sweet conference of the heart-confessed and other seen faults in the Assembly, to be remedied. Dr. Twisse closed with a short prayer and blessing. God was

so evidently in all this exercise that we expect certainly a blessing both
in our matter of the Assembly and the whole kingdom." The fervor of
this description almost causes the reader to ignore the tremendous
length of the exercise, even in a day when congregations begin to squirm
as a one-hour service draws to a close!

The members of the Westminster Assembly worked as hard as they
prayed. In the course of the five and a half years of its existence, the
convocation produced a remarkable series of documents pertaining to
the worship, government, and beliefs of the church. As each document
was produced, it was passed on to parliament as the "humble advice"
of the Assembly. Parliament did not rubber-stamp the work of the
Westminster divines, but took plenty of time to study and discuss each
piece of their report. Because of the significance of each of these documents to later generations of Presbyterians, it will be helpful for us to
review each of them, in the order in which they were completed and
passed on to the parliament.

The Directory for the Public Worship of God was completed in December, 1644, and approved by parliament in January, 1645. It was designed
to take the place of the Book of Common Prayer in the worship of the
church. It is significant to note that this was a "directory," or book of
directions or rubrics for public worship, rather than a "liturgy," which
would have provided the precise wording to be used. The Assembly
asserted (over against the Anglican practice) that the use of set forms
and prayers made for "an idle and unedifying Ministery [sic]" and thus
became "a matter of endlesse strife and contention in the church."

The Form of Church Government and Ordination was completed in
November, 1644, but was highly contested at every step, and not approved by parliament until 1648. This document set forth a presbyterian
form of government, with pastors, teachers, and "other church gover-
nors . . . [who] reformed churches generally call elders." It was designed
to take the place of the episcopal pattern which had been traditional in
the Church of England. The major opposition to the new plan, not only
in the Assembly but also in the parliament, came from those who
favored the congregational form.

The Psalter, which was a metrical version of the Psalms for use in public
worship, was finally approved by the Assembly after considerable revision in November, 1645. It was one of several competing versions which

had been considered, and happened to be the one submitted by Francis Rous, who was a member both of the Assembly and the parliament. *The Confession of Faith* was completed in December, 1646, and approved by parliament in March, 1648. *The Larger and Shorter Catechisms,* embodying the same theological system as the Confession in question and answer form, were completed in the fall of 1647, and approved by parliament in September, 1648. The three of these documents, taken together, represent the most impressive and lasting accomplishment of the Assembly. Three centuries later, they remain a basis for doctrinal orthodoxy among the vast majority of English-speaking Presbyterians.

The Church of England Becomes Presbyterian

When the parliament adopted these Westminster Standards just listed, the Church of England ceased to be episcopal and became presbyterian, at least in name. A great many Anglican ministers who were unwilling to accept presbyterian polity or Calvinist theology and worship were removed from their churches by parliamentary fiat. Still other ministers, Puritan to the core, had scruples concerning the proposed system of government, favoring the sort of congregational church government which was later to be known as the New England Way. Oliver Cromwell himself was opposed to presbyterian polity, and eventually purged the parliament of those who held such sentiments. In fine, although the Presbyterian Church had nominally become the established church in England, Presbyterianism did not lay hold of the hearts and minds of the great majority of the English people.

As the political circumstances of the nation shifted kaleidoscopically over the years following 1648, the presbyterian system was lost in the shuffle. As we have already seen, the attempt to establish the Commonwealth was destined to collapse soon after the death of Cromwell. In 1660 Charles II became king of England and Scotland, and soon episcopacy was restored as the manner of government of the Church of England.

The Disestablishment of English Presbyterianism

Charles and his supporters enacted rigid laws of conformity to the government and worship of the Church of England. Scotland's "killing time" was English Presbyterianism's time of great travail, too. About two thousand nonconforming Presbyterian ministers were ejected from their churches. Laws were passed forbidding them to live within five miles of their former churches or within five miles of an incorporated town. They were even forbidden to teach school, which was about the only viable livelihood to which they could turn.

Especially during the reigns of the later Stuart kings, Charles II and his brother James II, the Presbyterian Church in England was subjected to a struggle for its very existence. Even after the Revolution of 1688 that put William and Mary on the throne and ushered in the Toleration Act, Presbyterianism was barely tolerated. No presbyteries or synods were permitted, and every minister became a law unto himself. The English Presbyterian Church was weak, crippled, and plagued with dissent and heresy.

With the opening of the nineteenth century, however, there was an evangelical revival among the Presbyterians of England. This was partly due to the Methodist revival that had swept through England under the leadership of John Wesley, and partly due to the influence of Scottish Presbyterians who had settled in England. In 1876 there was a union of the various presbyterian groups, which yielded the modern Presbyterian Church of England. Today this denomination includes over 300 congregations and 60,000 members. Although it is far from the largest Presbyterian body in the world, its claim to lineal descent from the framers of the Westminster Standards gives it a place of special significance in the telling of our story. (In 1972 the Presbyterian Church of England merged with the Congregational Church in England and Wales to form the United Reformed Church.)

The Westminster Standards in Scotland

The irony of the failure of Presbyterianism in England after the monumental efforts of the Westminster divines is somewhat softened by the subsequent appreciation of their work in other places. Soon after the Assembly had finished its task, the Church of Scotland voted to lay aside its previous constitution, much of which dated back to the time of John Knox, and adopt the Confession of Faith, Catechisms, Book of Government, Directory of Worship, and Psalter which had been prepared at Westminster. This decision is all the more remarkable when we consider that the gathering had been composed of 121 English Puritan ministers and only 4 ministers from the Church of Scotland.

Certainly one reason for this decision was the intrinsic merit of the materials produced by Westminster. But the main reason for the change was the fact that the Scots believed their adoption of the Standards would promote more unity among the Presbyterians of England, Scotland, and Ireland. They had a vision of a great, unified Presbyterian Church, covering all three countries. Of course their vision was obscured by the disestablishment of the English church.

Nevertheless, their adoption of the Westminster Standards was a decision which had further impact than they would ever have dreamed possible. Subsequent generations of the church's life saw Scottish Presbyterians as bearers of this special tradition in their migrations and missions to Ireland, North America, Australia, New Zealand, and many of the nations of the Third World—literally to the uttermost parts of the earth.

Chapter Six

PRESBYTERIANISM
IN IRELAND

Irish Religion

No one knows precisely when or how Christianity first came to Ireland, but it must have arrived at a very early date. The early leadership of the Christian movement there is usually associated with the legendary Patrick, whose zeal for the Christian cause is said to have left its distinctive mark upon Ireland's culture (and ecology!) as well as its religion. The story of Patrick is so interwoven with heroic folktales that it is difficult to know what is history and what is legend, but it seems clear that he and other stalwart missionaries had made notable headway in the conversion of the Celtic tribes of Erin by the beginning of the fifth century.

Ireland was a land which was by-passed by the Protestant Reformation. Indeed, as it turned out, Roman Catholicism was more firmly entrenched in the hearts and lives of the natives of Ireland after the times of Luther and Calvin than it had been before. In the telling of the Presbyterian story, our interest in Irish religion has to do with some immigrant Scots—usually identified as "Scotch-Irish" or "Ulster Scots" —who sojourned there for a few generations before making their way to America. The story of their pilgrimage is a major key to the proper understanding of American Presbyterianism.

Ireland and the English Reformation

As we have mentioned in the previous chapter, in the year 1534 Henry VIII had the English parliament pass the Act of Supremacy, making him the head of the church in England and Ireland. England, of course, made the break from Catholicism fairly readily, but Ireland adamantly refused to accept the change. Eventually bolstered by the strong missionary activity of Jesuit priests, the Irish dug in their heels and determined to die rather than forsake the faith of their forebears. This insubordination to Henry's religious strategies was a source of constant conflict thereafter, erupting from time to time into open and bloody war between the Tudor rulers and the Irish. By the end of Elizabeth's reign in 1603, Ireland was a depopulated and barren land.

James I, who succeeded Elizabeth, openly admitted his inability to find a good solution for the Irish problem. He was impressed, however, by the advice offered by Francis Bacon, the philosopher and statesman. Bacon suggested that James use northern Ireland, which had been especially hard hit by the Tudor wars, as a settlement area for colonists from England and Scotland. Although earlier efforts to anglicize Ireland had failed, James became convinced that sufficient economic induce-ment could be built into the project to make it work. Consequently, he chartered what came to be known as "the Ulster Plantation," because it covered most of the Irish province of Ulster, and opened a program which entailed the offer of more and better farmland to rural tenants, at a rate which compared quite favorably with the rents they were paying in the rural areas of England and Scotland.

Most of the first settlers came from the lowland counties of Scot-land and the adjacent English border counties, where there had been constant feuding during the times before the union of the two nations under James. James must have felt that he was killing two birds with one stone by reducing the friction along the ancient border at the same time that he was sending loyal and hardy Protestant settlers into a Catholic trouble spot in the north of Ireland. Upon their arrival, the newcomers quite literally drove most of the remaining Irish population from the land, and began to develop a lifestyle which was far more prosperous than that which they had left behind.

It is significant to notice that James was beginning this project in Ireland just at the time when religious sentiments in England and Scotland were reaching their peak. The lowland Scots, who were by far the majority of the new settlers, were products of the Reformed ethos which had been initiated by Knox and his successors. At first, it is likely that their religious sentiments were not very much involved in their decision to colonize. Later, however, when James and his son, Charles I, began to press for conformity to the worship and government of the Church of England, the Ulster Plantation came to be a sort of safety valve for religious dissent.

From the very first, there was a natural antagonism between the native Irish inhabitants and the Scottish settlers. It is often said that the term "Scotch-Irish," which we often use for those settlers, is something of a misnomer, if we take it to imply a mixture of Scottish and Irish blood lines. There seems to have been a minimal amount of intermarriage between the two groups. At times, there was actually legal restriction of such practice; the rest of the time, religious and cultural differences aggravated the initial hostility between the new landholders and those whom they had dispossessed.

The Planting of Presbyterianism in Ulster

It would be a mistake to suppose that all of these "Ulster Scots" were cultured, pious Presbyterians. Although the picture should not be overdrawn, it seems clear that for the most part they were rough-hewn men and women who were leaving behind a marginal existence as tenants in the Scottish lowlands in order to better themselves in a new circumstance. Some of the more pious among them were obviously appalled at the lack of religious commitment on the part of the majority. Andrew Stewart, a Presbyterian who lived and worked among the early settlers of Ulster Plantation, was inclined to think of his fellow pioneers as "generally the scum of both nations." He wrote: "Most of the people were void of all godliness, who seemed rather to flee from God in their enterprise, than to follow their own mercy. Yet God followed them when they fled from Him. Albeit, at first, it must be remembered, that they cared little for any church, so God seemed to care as little for them."

Stewart was among a stalwart group of Scottish pastors, however, who undertook to change the religious complexion of the settlement. The presence of these ministers, according to one modern interpreter of the Ulster experience, was a considerable factor in the success of the Scottish effort. "By their efforts with the transplanted Scottish farmers," writes James Leyburn, "there achieved a kind of second Reformation among the Scots of Ulster and gave the people the sense of having their dearest institution at hand."

As has happened in many other situations, some of these missionary pastors were men of little promise—at least from the vantage of worldly talent—who nevertheless wrought great things. Pastor James Glendinning, for example, was judged by a contemporary to be "a man who would never have been chosen by a wise assembly of ministers, nor sent to begin a reformation in this land, for he was little better than distracted, yea, afterwards, did actually distract. Yet this was the Lord's choice to begin the admirable work of God, which I mention on purpose, that all men may see how the glory is only the Lord's in making a holy nation in this profane land, and that it was not by might nor by power, nor by man's wisdom, but by the Spirit of the Lord." Thus a great revival was brought about among the Scottish settlers in Ulster through men of common gifts.

Pressures of Persecution

The religious commitments which were rekindled among the Scots in northern Ireland were sorely tested during the era of the Puritan Revolution in England. Charles I, who laid such a heavy hand of persecution upon the Puritans in England and the Presbyterians in Scotland, was no less severe in his dealings with dissenters in Ireland. In 1633, the same year in which he appointed William Laud to be Archbishop of Canterbury, Charles chose the notorious Thomas Wentworth (later Lord Strafford) to be Lord Deputy of Ireland. A major part of Wentworth's duty was to see that the native Roman Catholics of southern Ireland and the immigrant Presbyterians of northern Ireland aligned themselves with the practices and theology of the Church of England.

Wentworth required the Scots in Ulster to take an oath "upon the Holy Evangelists" that they would give their full allegiance to Charles I, that they would not at any time oppose anything that he might command, and that they would renounce and abjure all Scottish Covenants (specifically, of course, the great National Covenant repudiating Anglican worship). It is no wonder that Wentworth's demand soon came to be known as the Black Oath.

Great numbers of the transplanted Scots refused to take the oath. Many were imprisoned, and many more went into hiding. Others chose to "commute" to Scotland to receive communion in proper fashion, while still others decided to give up the colonial venture altogether, in order to return home to the nation which was girding itself for war against Charles. The loyalist Wentworth set to work raising an army in Ireland, comprised primarily of native Catholics, in order to give assistance to the king. Before he could lead them into action, though, he was recalled to England by Charles and his army was nominally disbanded. The Ulster Scots viewed his departure as a blessing, and some even considered his execution at parliamentary order the next year to be a matter of divine retribution.

Even after the departure of Wentworth, however, the Presbyterians in Ireland did not gain any real reprieve from their suffering. In 1641, the seething discontent of the native Irish erupted into open warfare against the Scottish settlers. The army which had been raised by Wentworth to support the royalist cause became the nucleus for the native Irish uprising. The fighting continued for over a decade, during which time the Scots and English in Ireland were increasingly hard-pressed to maintain a foothold in their adopted land. England was preoccupied with its own Civil War, and thus unable or unwilling to intervene until 1649, when Parliament dispatched an army of ten thousand men to bring peace. Cromwell himself came to Ireland in 1650, and established parliamentary control in decisive if violent fashion. Some contemporary estimates indicated that more than a third of the Irish population, Protestant and Catholic, died of the fighting and privations of this time.

Presbyterianism in Northern Ireland

As can well be imagined, early attempts to establish a presbyterian system of church organization in Ulster were severely hindered by the instability of the political situation. In June of 1642, the first presbytery was organized at the town of Carrickfergus, just north of Belfast, composed of five ministers and four elders. A decade later, there were still only a half dozen Presbyterian ministers in all of northern Ireland. The arrival of the parliamentary army in 1649 brought renewed hope for the cause, however, for many of the soldiers were Scottish Presbyterians, and each regiment had a sort of presbyterian session drawn from among the ranks. For this and other reasons, growth came fairly rapidly after the peace was established. By 1660 there were eighty Presbyterian congregations, seventy ministers, five presbyteries, and almost 100,000 communicants in northern Ireland.

Even the restoration of a Stuart king, Charles II, did not initially bring the sort of hard times in Ulster Plantation which might have been expected. Several dozen ministers were deprived of state support as a result of the Act of Uniformity in 1660, but most of them were allowed to continue their pastoral duties. Charles' obvious concentration on affairs in England spared the Scots in Ireland from the "killing times" faced by their Covenanter cousins at home, and the migrations from the homeland to Ireland in quest of peace and religious toleration increased remarkably during Charles' reign. The revocation of the Edict of Nantes in France in 1685 also added a considerable number of Huguenots to the Protestant population of northern Ireland.

It was the termination of Stuart control of England that next brought peril to Irish Protestantism. When the pro-Catholic James II was driven from the English throne and replaced by William and Mary in 1688, a new crisis occurred. James, who fled at first to France, came to Ireland with an army in order to seek Catholic support for an invasion of England. Almost at once he led his Frenchmen against the Protestants in the north, in order to bring the whole island into his column. William also sent his armies to Ireland, and Ulster once again became the battleground. The stories of the siege of Londonderry and the battle at the River Boyne constitute thrilling chapters in the history of Scotch-Irish Presbyterians. At the Boyne, James was completely routed. He fled to France, and William and Mary were firmly established on the English throne. William's Act of Toleration provided the basis for another period of Presbyterian growth and prosperity in Ulster. By his death in 1702, there were nine presbyteries, 120 congregations, and over a hundred ministers.

The Great Migration

When William died, Anne, the daughter of James II, came to the British throne. Though certainly not as hostile to Presbyterianism as her father had been, Anne caused the Ulster Presbyterians a great deal of difficulty by directing the passage of the so-called Test Act. By this statute, all persons holding public office in Ireland were required to take communion in the Church of England within three months after election or appointment to office. Obviously, most Ulster Scots in positions of authority were forced from office by this act, since they considered Anglican sacramentalism to be only a small step this side of Catholicism.

The situation was further complicated by the imposition of economic sanctions of various sorts which placed Irish commercial interests at a distinct disadvantage in the world of trade. In addition, the institution of a renegotiation of land-leases in Ulster, by what was known as the "rack-rent" system, forced many Scottish settlers there to relinquish choice properties they had held since their migration. To add woe upon woe, Ulster then experienced a series of drought years, attended by an especially pernicious smallpox epidemic.

Under this conspiracy of circumstances, the Scottish Presbyterians in northern Ireland began to make their way to the British colonies in North America in large numbers. Between 1717 and 1775 there were five noticeable waves of immigrants, with lesser numbers in the intervening periods. A reasonable estimate of the number involved in this movement would be somewhere in the neighborhood of a quarter of a million people. Settling primarily in southeastern Pennsylvania, the Valley of Virginia, and the Carolina piedmont, these people provided the strong backbone of Presbyterian sentiment in the colonies as they moved toward their struggle for independence.

Presbyterianism in Ireland Today

In Northern Ireland today there are about 150,000 communing Presbyterians, with more than five hundred churches and ministers. A comparison of these figures with those given above for the year 1660 gives the impression that the numerical growth over the period of three centuries has been modest; but we must not overlook the hundreds of thousands of Ulster Presbyterians who emigrated to America and other lands, to strengthen and enrich the Presbyterian tradition in those places.

Sad to say, another fact to be recalled is the heritage of strife which has haunted Irish religion ever since the time of the Reformation. It is not without significance that the center of Presbyterianism in that land is Belfast, the embattled city whose agony has been international news for more than a decade. It is also sad, but necessary, to confess that

Presbyterians in Northern Ireland have sometimes been a part of the problem as well as the solution in that place where people are striving to learn to live as brothers and sisters.

If one assesses the significance of the Irish Presbyterian heritage, perhaps the most significant feature is the tenacity of these people, and their willingness to suffer in the name of their faith. As in many other lands, Presbyterianism in Ireland continues to be a minority movement. The very existence of this church is a testimony to the faith upon which it has been founded and sustained.

Chapter Seven

PRESBYTERIANISM IN AMERICA; THE UNITED PRESBYTERIAN CHURCH IN THE U.S.A.

Presbyterians Come to America

The settlement of the portion of North America which was later to become the United States was dominated by immigrants who were committed to the Reformed heritage. It is generally estimated that as many as three out of every four Americans at the time of the Revolutionary War were directly or indirectly products of Calvinism.

This is not to say, of course, that all of them were Presbyterians. Indeed, the dominance of the congregational way among the New Englanders and the genuinely flexible attitude of many settlers in other colonies with regard to church polity have made it rather difficult for subsequent historians to pinpoint the precise beginnings of Presbyterianism in our land. The feature that we see with greatest clarity at the outset is the rich diversity of European backgrounds which flow into the life of the Presbyterian community in the New World. The stories we have told in the previous chapters converge into the drama which unfolds in America. Consider the variety:

Among the Puritans who settled in New England, there were at least a few who had a decided preference for presbyterian church government. It has been said, with considerable justification, that the sort of compromise which was attained in the congregationalism of the colony of Connecticut, in which there was a gathering of congregations into presbytery-like associations, provided one basis for the growth of our sort of polity in later times.

There were many other Calvinists who came to the New World at about the same time as the Puritans. The Dutch, for instance, began to settle New Netherlands (later New York) and established the Dutch Reformed Church, presbyterian in everything but name, as the official church of the colony.

The French Huguenots, fleeing the constant persecutions of their native land, also began to arrive in America at an early date. Some settled in New England, others in New York, still others in Virginia, South Carolina, and Georgia. Some of them became Anglicans in their adopted land, but the majority eventually came into the Presbyterian church.

A large body of German settlers also came to America in colonial times, and although many were Lutheran, a fair number of them were Calvinists and Presbyterians. Most of them settled in Pennsylvania, or drifted south into the Valley of Virginia and the piedmont Carolinas. The majority of these Calvinist Germans eventually became the German Reformed Church, but through the years many have entered the Presbyterian Church.

Many Scottish Presbyterians came to America directly from Scotland in early colonial days. They settled in New Jersey, the Carolinas, and other colonies, and had a large part in laying the foundations of American Presbyterianism.

Perhaps the largest single group of Presbyterians, as we have seen, were those who arrived from Northern Ireland. These Scotch-Irish or Ulster Scots began to migrate to America in the second decade of the eighteenth century. Entering the new land at various places, they tended to move toward the frontiers. Some who settled in Pennsylvania made their way westward as far as Pittsburgh, and laid the foundations of that great city. Others went south from Pennsylvania into the Valley of Virginia, and on into North Carolina. Those who landed at Charleston made their way to the northwest, into the piedmont area. The two streams met in Mecklenburg County, North Carolina, and York County, South Carolina, making these two the most thoroughly Scotch-Irish counties in the South.

Organizing Presbyterianism in America

All of these strands of Presbyterianism came together in the American colonial situation in unpremeditated fashion. Except for the case of the Dutch, there was virtually no official sanction or encouragement, insofar as presbyterian polity was concerned. If the faithful intended to be organized in that fashion, they clearly had to do it themselves.

It is hard to say when and where the first avowedly Presbyterian church was founded in America. The honor may well belong to the congregation formed at Jamaica, Long Island, in 1672. It was not until the opening of the eighteenth century, however, that there was an inter-congregational structure based upon government by elders. Its establishment was due to the efforts of the man who stands above all others in the story of our American beginnings: Francis Makemie.

Makemie has justly been called "the Father of American Presbyterianism." An Ulster Scot, he was ordained by the Presbytery of Laggan in Northern Ireland in 1683, and came at once to America. He was only twenty-five, but he had a genius for leadership and organization. In his early years in America, he was forced to pursue a "tent-making" ministry as a merchant-missionary in order to make a living. All the while, though, he was organizing Presbyterian churches on the eastern shore of Maryland, and travelling up and down the seaboard giving encouragement to scattered Presbyterians.

Makemie went to England in 1704 to recruit other Presbyterian clergymen for the tiny American congregations. Shortly after his return, he gathered a group, consisting of seven ministers and "certain elders," for the purpose of constituting the first American presbytery. The place and date of that first meeting are not definitely known. Makemie simply tells us that it was "a meeting of ministers for ministerial exercise to consult the most proper measures for advancing religion and propagating Christianity." That was the beginning of organized Presbyterianism in America.

Makemie's name is also connected with the struggle for religious freedom in the colonies. While preaching in New York, he and a colleague were imprisoned by Lord Cornbury, the royal governor, for preaching without permission. At the trial, Makemie ably defended himself against the governor's charges, demonstrating that it was the governor himself who had flouted the law, by ignoring the plain stipulations of the Act of Toleration. He was acquitted, and Cornbury was recalled to England soon thereafter, partly because of the sort of high-handedness he had shown in dealing with Makemie.

Francis Makemie and his early companions were untiring in their efforts to organize a Presbyterian community in the British colonies. Within less than a decade after his death in 1708, the stage was set for a further development in church organization in America. In 1717 the American Presbytery reorganized itself into a synod, to be comprised of four member presbyteries: Long Island, Philadelphia, New Castle, and Snow Hill. At the first meeting of the new synod, which was named the Synod of Philadelphia, there were seventeen ministers and a number of ruling elders present. At the time there were only nineteen ministers, forty churches, and about three thousand communicants within the American Presbyterian communion.

Tensions Within Presbyterianism

Not long after the organization of the synod, a sharp controversy arose as to whether ministers should be required to subscribe to all the doctrines of the Westminster Confession of Faith and Catechisms. Up to that time there had been no such requirement. In general, ministers of Scottish and Scotch-Irish descent were in favor of strict subscription to those standards. Those of English background were typically opposed to it.

A compromise was finally reached, and in 1729 the Synod of Philadelphia approved a measure known as the Adopting Act, by which the Westminster Confession and Catechisms were established as the official doctrinal statements of American Presbyterianism. Ministers were required to subscribe to these standards as "being in all the essential and necessary articles, good forms of sound words and systems of Christian doctrine." If any minister had any scruples about accepting anything in the Confession or Catechisms, he was to make his reservations to the presbytery or synod, so that it might judge if any essential or necessary doctrine was involved in his dissent. If it was decided that the matter did in fact touch upon an essential aspect of the faith, then the minister was expected to withdraw from the Presbyterian ministry. If, on the other hand, the minister differed only on a matter that was adjudged non-essential, then the members of the body agreed "that none of us will traduce or use any opprobrious terms of those who differ from us in these extra-essential and not necessary points of doctrine, but treat them with the same friendship, kindness and brotherly love, as if they had not differed from us in such sentiments."

Such a generous and open settlement might have provided a broad basis for fellowship within the church had it not been for that wave of religious sentiment we call the Great Awakening, which swept over the American colonies in the decade following the Adopting Act. Although the Awakening had profound influence for good among Americans, it also aroused a spirit of controversy within several of the major religious groups in the colonies. Among the Presbyterians, the dispute was between parties which came to be called the "Old Side" and the "New Side." The Old Side was opposed to revivalism, as exemplified by the Awakening, because of the emotionalism and potential disorder in the movement. The New Side responded that the Old Side opposition was engendered by a spiritual deadness within its ranks. Gilbert Tennent, a young New Side pastor, preached and published a sermon entitled "The Danger of an Unconverted Ministry," which was a rather uncharitable denunciation of all pastors who opposed the revivals.

Another closely related issue was the debate over the proper mode of education for the ministry. As the population grew apace and conversions brought more people into the churches, the question of securing an adequate supply of pastors was a major concern. The Old Side group believed that ministers for the American churches should be educated in the fashion which had become traditional in the universities of the Old World and New England. The New Side adherents felt that this was both slow and unsuitable. Accordingly, they had begun to build schools for the education of ministers. William Tennent, father of Gilbert Tennent, had built one such school, derisively called "the Log College" by the Old Side group, which was a lineal ancestor of Princeton University.

This dispute over education combined with the other issues growing out of the revival to produce a crisis in American Presbyterianism. The censorious spirit of the younger Tennent's sermon was soon matched by the attitude of the opposition. At the meeting of the synod in 1741, the Old Side majority declared that the Presbytery of New Brunswick, of which most of the New Side revivalists were members, was no longer a part of the Synod of Philadelphia. Four years later, that presbytery joined with two other New Side presbyteries to form the Synod of New York. Thus there came to be two Presbyterian synods in colonial America, split apart by controversy when there were still not more than ten thousand members of the denomination in all the colonies, and when a growing population and spirit of religious interest called loudly for united action.

This first of several painful divisions in American Presbyterianism did not last interminably, however; in 1758 the two synods were able to reunite, on the basis of a compromise on the issues which had caused the differences of opinion. The reunited church called itself the Synod of New York and Philadelphia, and consisted of almost one hundred ministers, two hundred churches, and more than ten thousand members.

Geographical Expansion

Our discussion thus far has hinted that Presbyterianism depended for its strength and vitality primarily upon the people who settled the middle colonies: New York, New Jersey, Pennsylvania, and Delaware. Although this is generally true, it is significant to note also that Presbyterians were able to do some very effective "home mission" work in the colonial period, especially in the Southern colonies. Even during the time of the Old Side-New Side split, the work in the South proceeded, largely under the auspices of young and vigorous New Side clergymen.

The most notable of these itinerants was the Reverend Samuel Davies, who came to Hanover County, Virginia (near Richmond) in 1747. A product of the Log College, Davies was only twenty-four years of age at the time of his coming into Virginia as a missionary from the Presbytery of New Castle. He secured permission from the colonial government to preach at several stations in Virginia, some more than a hundred miles apart. Although physically frail, Davies was a preacher of remarkable power. Patrick Henry is said to have declared that he was the most eloquent speaker he had ever heard. In 1755, under the leadership of Davies, Hanover Presbytery was organized, with general responsibility for everything south of the Potomac River. This represented the beginning of organized Presbyterianism in the South. Davies left Virginia in 1759 to accept the presidency of Princeton, but died two years later at the age of thirty-eight.

Another New Side evangelist, Alexander Craighead, began to do pioneer mission work for the Presbyterians in the Valley of Virginia in 1749. In 1757 he moved south into piedmont North Carolina, where he became the pastor of the Rocky River Church, not far from present-day Charlotte. From there he covered a great deal of territory, laying the foundations for organized Presbyterianism in that part of the country.

After the reunion of the "sides" in 1758, the expansion of the church proceeded with increased enthusiasm. In several places, Christian schools were established which were to blossom into colleges of a later generation. Presbyterians began to place emphasis upon the importance of missionary work among the Indians, and efforts were made to produce and distribute Christian literature among the Southern settlers.

The American Revolution

The involvement of Presbyterians in the war for American independence is a story of legendary proportions. From the English point of view, the revolution was sometimes perceived as a "Presbyterian rebellion." Indeed, one disgusted Loyalist grumbled that the American colonies had "run off with a Presbyterian parson!" Almost to a man, the Presbyterian clergy in America took up the patriot cause, and provided warm support for the cause of liberty from their pulpits.

It can be said that they were animated in part by the persistent fear of the imposition of resident bishops by the Church of England, a change which would have seriously undercut Presbyterian growth, especially in the South. But it is more to the point to say that Presbyterian theology has never mixed easily with the arbitrary nature of monarchical government. The social-contract theory in which the founding fathers of the new nation found their justification for the rebellion has sometimes been nicknamed "political Calvinism." At least it made abundant good sense to those steeped in the Presbyterian tradition.

Of even greater significance, perhaps, than the Presbyterian support of the patriot cause in time of war, is the way in which our church was involved in the setting of the course for the future, once independence was a reality. But we must be modest. It is entirely too much to claim, as some have done, that our American system of government is based upon the Presbyterian system. Better say that both understandings of human organization derive from the same cultural milieu, which has the Calvinist-Puritan heritage as one of its most significant components.

It is not too much to claim some credit, though, for Presbyterians —among many others—as framers of the unique system of church and state which we Americans enjoy. Those who suspected Presbyterians of intending to become the "establishment" of the new nation possessed little awareness of the traditional Reformed mistrust of such privilege. As the war was drawing to a close, the Synod of New York and Philadelphia placed itself on record as favoring the principle "that every peaceable member of civil society ought to be protected in the full and free exercise of their religion."

The First General Assembly

While statesmen were preparing a constitution for the new United States of America, churchmen were planning the organization of a General Assembly which would include all the Presbyterian churches in the new nation. To this end the Synod of New York and Philadelphia, in May of 1788, divided itself into four synods, composed of a total of sixteen presbyteries. The four synods were: the Synod of New York and New Jersey, the Synod of Philadelphia, the Synod of Virginia, and the Synod of the Carolinas. Each body was directed to meet at a certain time and place, in order to pave the way for a meeting of the new General Assembly for the first time during the following year. Steps were taken to amend the portions of the Westminster Standards that needed to be changed in order to apply to the conditions of the American situation.

The first meeting of the new General Assembly was held in Philadelphia in May, 1789, just three weeks after George Washington was inaugurated as the first president of the nation. The assembly adopted the name "the General Assembly of the Presbyterian Church in the United States of America," thus testifying to its intention to be a church of national scope and vision. There were over four hundred churches and twenty thousand communicants in the new denomination, as well as 177 ordained pastors.

At the time of the organization of the new General Assembly, the Presbyterians probably occupied the most advantageous position of any religious group in America. There were several reasons for this. For one thing, their church had been almost unanimous in its support of the patriot cause, and thus enjoyed the honor of the victorious effort. Moreover, the membership of the church included a high proportion of the most able and influential citizens in many local situations. Beyond that, the church could boast an educated clergy, a well-articulated organizational structure, and several institutions of learning. The church was now thoroughly organized, and thoroughly committed to the expansion of the new nation. With all of these elements combining, Presbyterianism faced the future of the new nation with the same sort of optimism that typified the national mood.

A Cooperative Union

Although there seems to have been a period of spiritual lethargy immediately following the revolutionary years, there was also a remarkable revival of religion during the last years of the eighteenth century which set the stage for several decades of vigorous religious expansion, sometimes labelled the "Second Great Awakening." Most of the major religious groups in America were very much involved in the new fervor, and the Presbyterians were certainly no exception.

In 1801 the Presbyterian and Congregationalist Churches entered into an official policy of comity and cooperation in new areas of work, which was known as the Plan of Union. Ministers from each denomination would be accepted as pastors in congregations belonging to the other, and some congregations were allowed to hold a sort of joint membership in both denominations at the same time. The purpose of the plan, of course, was to enable both of these Reformed denominations to keep abreast of the needs for missionary work among the settlers in the rapidly growing area beyond the Appalachians. Thousands of people were emigrating from the older settlements along the Atlantic seaboard to "the West": Ohio, Indiana, Kentucky, Tennessee, and western New York. Neither denomination had a sufficient number of ministers to keep up with the explosion of new settlement by itself, so the two willingly joined hands.

From the Presbyterian point of view, the plan worked admirably insofar as numbers and geographical coverage was concerned. During the thirty-five years after the Plan of Union was adopted, Presbyterianism had a remarkable growth spurt. The best statistics available indicate that in 1800 the denomination had 180 ministers, 449 churches, and about twenty thousand members. In 1837, it had 2,140 ministers, 2,965 churches, and 220,000 members. Thus in some respects, it had grown better than tenfold in a little more than a generation.

This rapid growth was partially due to the great frontier revivals which typified the Second Great Awakening. In Kentucky and Tennessee, for example, the influx of new converts was so overwhelming that even the united efforts of Congregationalists and Presbyterians could not begin to provide sufficient pastoral leadership to organize and care for the new Christians. This was the time when the Baptists and Methodists, with their flexibility of organization and ministerial training, seized the initiative. Some Presbyterians wanted to lower the standards of education for the ministry and loosen the connection between American Presbyterianism and the Calvinism of the Westminster Standards, which was not as compatible with revivalism as a more Arminian stance might have been. A sharp controversy arose, which resulted in the withdrawal of some Presbyterians to form the Cumberland Presbyterian Church in 1810. Even after the Cumberland split, other points of disagreement continued to plague the Presbyterian community in the early decades of the nineteenth century.

The Old School-New School Controversy

Although the Plan of Union with the Congregationalists worked well—indeed to the advantage of the Presbyterians—insofar as the growth of the denomination was concerned, problems began to emerge which threatened the continuation of the liaison. For one thing, it was not long until questions were raised as to the theological views of some of the Congregationalist-trained ministers who were preaching in Presbyterian churches. Some feared that they were prophets of a "New Divinity"—a sort of attenuated Calvinism which would lead the people astray. In addition to this theological dispute, there were numerous conflicts within the denomination over the best ways to organize, regulate, and finance the missionary effort. Once again, parties developed within the American Presbyterian church. One party, known as the Old School, advocated a rigid adherence to the Calvinism of Westminster and a tight control of all missionary activity by the denomination itself. In general, the members of the Old School faction were also eager to avoid embroiling the church in the controversy over the major social issue of the day: the problem of slavery. The other party, known as the New School, believed in a measure of theological latitude, and favored interdenominational cooperation in missions, even at the expense of some theological niceties. The New School was also increasingly identified with the anti-slavery cause, and thus had most of its support in the North.

The breach between the two parties became wider and wider with the passing years. In the General Assembly of 1837, the Old School enjoyed a sufficient majority to pass a resolution which declared that the 1801 Plan of Union with the Congregational Church had been unconstitutional from the beginning, and that all that had been done under that agreement was therefore null and void. One immediate result of this decision was the amputation of four western synods which had been organized under the plan. This action split the Presbyterian Church almost half in two, with each group becoming a separate denomination. The Old School had about 120,000 members, distributed fairly evenly throughout the Northeast and the South. The New School had about 100,000 members, many of whom were in the areas of frontier growth, and only about 10,000 of whom were in the South. The division was a severe blow to Presbyterian prospects in a nation which was also moving toward a time of great distress.

Sectional Divisions and the Civil War

After the division into Old and New School Churches, neither Presbyterian group grew very rapidly. As the war clouds gathered, all of the major religious denominations in the land suffered unbelieveable tensions. In 1844–45, for example, both the Baptist and Methodist Churches split into Northern and Southern denominations over the matter of slavery. In 1857 the New School Presbyterian Assembly passed some forthright resolutions condemning slavery, whereupon the Southern minority of that church withdrew and organized yet another small Presbyterian denomination, which called itself "The United Synod of the South."

The Old School General Assembly, exercising a sort of invisible "gag rule" on the issue of slavery, managed to maintain its unity until after hostilities had actually broken out in 1861. It was at the General Assembly of that fateful year, though, that the Reverend Gardiner Spring of New York offered resolutions calling upon Presbyterians, North and South, to "strengthen, uphold and encourage the Federal government" in its efforts against the states which had seceded and formed the Confederate States of America. When the Spring resolutions were adopted, the Southern commissioners withdrew, and the church was divided. On December 4, 1861, at the city of Augusta, Georgia, "The General Assembly of the Presbyterian Church in the Confederate States of America" came into being.

At the beginning of 1837 there had been one Presbyterian Church in the United States of America. By the close of 1861 that church had split into four branches, each of which constituted a separate and distinct denomination.

The Presbyterian Church in the U.S.A.

The terrible days of the Civil War were hard on Presbyterians in all of these denominations. In the subsequent chapter we shall turn to the story of the church in the South. Here we shall briefly summarize the post-Civil War experience of the Northern church, which was soon to resume the name, "The Presbyterian Church in the United States of America."

In 1870 the Old School North and the New School North were reunited amid great rejoicing. At the same time, an invitation was extended to the Presbyterians in the South to reunite with their brothers and sisters in the North, but they declined. The reunited Northern church grew up with the developing nation after the war. As the population of the Western states and territories burgeoned, the church followed the migration with an aggressive policy of home missions. Even the South was involved in these missionary plans, especially through the educational ministry of schools and colleges for Southern blacks. The church also developed its foreign mission program significantly during the latter-nineteenth century, earning the reputation as one of the greatest missionary churches in the world.

In 1903 the Presbyterian Church in the U.S.A. enacted some moderate revisions to the Westminster Confession of Faith. Two chapters were added to the confession, and an explanatory statement was added as a means of interpreting the chapter on the decrees of God. Although there were tensions in the church over theological issues, the historic commitment of the denomination to the Reformed tradition remained basically intact.

After the revision of the Confession, the Presbyterian Church
U.S.A. issued an invitation to all Presbyterian bodies in America to unite
and thus form one great American Presbyterian Church. The Cumberland Presbyterian Church, which had split off from the mainstream in
1810, voted to accept the invitation, and in 1906 reunited with the
Presbyterian Church U.S.A. on the basis of the revised Confession. Sad
to say, the union was not perfect, since about one-third of the members
of the Cumberland Church refused to go into the union.

In 1957 the Presbyterian Church U.S.A. and the United Presbyterian Church, a smaller denomination with roots running back to the
Covenanters and Seceders in Scotland, voted to merge under the combined name "The United Presbyterian Church in the United States of
America." Again at that time, other Presbyterian bodies declined the
invitation to enter the union; but the opportunity for merger remains
open down to the present day.

In 1967, after years of preparation, the United Presbyterian
Church U.S.A. acted to enlarge the confessional basis of the church's
life. For the first time since the Adopting Act of 1729, it came to pass
that the Westminster Standards were not the only doctrinal basis for the
major American Presbyterian body. The General Assembly and a large
majority of its member presbyteries voted to adopt a book of confessions
as the doctrinal standards for the denomination. The book includes the
Westminster Confession, of course, but it also includes other excellent
representations of the Christian tradition, such as the Apostles' Creed,
the Nicene Creed, the Scots Confession of 1560, and the Heidelberg
Catechism of 1563. One of the documents, the so-called Confession of
1967, was especially written for inclusion, as a witness to the meaning
of our faith in the modern day. Together, the nine statements of faith
in this book now constitute the doctrinal basis for that denomination's
life and work.

In recent years the United Presbyterian Church U.S.A. has shown
tremendous vitality. It has contributed outstanding leadership to the
ecumenical movement and has taken courageous, self-sacrificing stands
in matters of human justice and world peace. With over two and a half
million communicant members, it remains the largest Presbyterian communion in the world.

Chapter Eight
THE PRESBYTERIAN CHURCH
IN THE UNITED STATES

The United Heritage

The story we have surveyed in the previous chapter demonstrates the fact that the vast majority of American Presbyterians were originally together in one national denomination. Time and circumstance brought divisions, only some of which have been resolved, in that united witness. In a subsequent chapter, we will have occasion to survey the multiplicity of smaller Presbyterian bodies in America, as well as our kindred denominations in other places throughout the world.

In the present chapter, though, we need to consider the story of the denomination of which many of the readers of this book are members, which came into being at the time of the division of the American nation. As we have seen, the tragedy which divided the North and South in the great Civil War was one which touched religious life as surely and as painfully as it did the other aspects of the national experience.

Initially, the new church in the seceding states took the name "The Presbyterian Church in the Confederate States of America." At the close of the war, of course, the name was changed to "The Presbyterian Church in the United States," the name which it still bears today. (Those who have trouble recalling our official title find it helpful to remember that "U.S." spells "us.") Sometimes our denomination is called "The Southern Presbyterian Church," but that is not its official name. In fact, the General Assembly of 1865 rather decisively rejected the suggestion that the new name be "The Presbyterian Church of the South."

It is attractive to suppose that one reason for this decision was the recognition that the heritage of our denomination stretches far beyond the bitter struggle which had just closed. As an integral part of the American Presbyterian movement from its colonial beginnings, our church has a full share in all the history of that community prior to 1861. Since we have already traced that story in the previous chapter, let us merely summarize the portion of it which relates to the South before bringing the story of the separate denomination up to date.

Presbyterianism in the Antebellum South

As early as 1640 there were scatterings of English Puritans with Presbyterian leanings on the eastern shore of Virginia and Maryland. A few Ulster Scots settled in Virginia in the latter half of the seventeenth century, and many more came there, and into the piedmont Carolinas before the outbreak of the Revolution. Presbyterians directly from Scotland settled in the Carolina tidewater area at an early date, and after the revocation of the Edict of Nantes a great many French Huguenots came to Virginia, South Carolina, and Georgia. During the eighteenth century, there was even a movement of some Calvinists of Swiss and German descent into the Southern colonies. Thus there was a great deal of raw material available to Presbyterianism in the South; the major ingredient lacking among these settlers was organization.

Francis Makemie began to organize churches on the eastern shore of Maryland in 1684. The French Huguenots began to develop congregations in and around Charleston just a few years later. In the Valley of Virginia the Presbyterians began to organize congregations about 1730. Samuel Davies began his great work around Richmond in 1747. From 1750 on, evangelists were busy organizing churches in North Carolina. Thus the beginnings of Southern Presbyterianism were developing along several different lines in the pre-Revolutionary period.

In 1755 the Presbytery of Hanover, which generally embraced everything south of the Potomac River, was organized by the Synod of New York. The Synod of New York, you will recall, was the "New Side" or evangelistic faction of the split which had developed in 1741 over differing attitudes toward revivalism. The pro-revival Synod of New York thus did most of the evangelistic and organizational work in the South during the years of division. When the two "sides" were reunited in 1758, there was already a strong footing for Presbyterian development in the Southern colonies. Orange Presbytery, consisting of everything south of Virginia, was constituted in 1770.

After the Revolutionary War, as the Synod of New York and Philadelphia resolved itself into the new General Assembly, two of the four synods it projected were located in the South. The Synod of Virginia, consisting of four presbyteries, held its first meeting at New Providence Church, in the Valley of Virginia, on October 22, 1788. Just two weeks later, on November 5, the Synod of the Carolinas, with three member presbyteries, convened at old Centre Church, near what was later to be the site of Davidson College.

As the early pioneers pushed the frontiers further to the South and West, the Presbyterian Church followed, organizing churches, presbyteries, and synods throughout the new territory. Although usually outnumbered by the Baptists and Methodists, and occasionally beset by internal dissension, such as the Cumberland schism in Kentucky and Tennessee, our denomination provided a unique witness in the new areas of the South. Among the more noteworthy aspects of their activity were the pioneering efforts in the area of education, with many Presbyterian pastors serving as the schoolmasters and founders of colleges on the frontier. In addition, a handful of Presbyterian pastors were active in trying to alleviate the plight of the Southern Indians, even risking imprisonment for the sake of their rights. Other pastors, such as the Reverend Charles Colcock Jones of Liberty County, Georgia, led efforts to provide religious instruction for the slave population of the Southern states. Presbyterian growth in the region was slow but steady. By 1860 there were twelve synods, 1,275 churches, and nearly one hundred thousand Presbyterian communicants in the Southern and border states.

The Impact of the Civil War

It has been said that one of the most durable sources of the continued union of our nation in the troublous years before 1861 was the Old School wing of the Presbyterian Church. It is indeed a remarkable fact that this one denomination managed to hold together through all the controversies about slavery and secession up until May of 1861. The Methodist and Baptist communions had divided North and South over slavery in 1844-45. The New School Presbyterians, rather sparsely represented in the South, had gone the same route in 1857. Among the denominations with substantial Southern participation, only the Old School Presbyterian group was left intact after hostilities began.

When the General Assembly of the undivided church met in Philadelphia on May 16, 1861, eight states had already seceded, the Confederate States of America was a political reality, and the national bloodbath had begun. Needless to say, the atmosphere was tense, even though only a few Southern commissioners were actually in attendance at the assembly. On the sixth day of the meeting, after prolonged discussion, the historic Gardiner Spring Resolutions in support of the Federal cause were adopted by a vote of 156 to 66.

The next steps were entirely inevitable. There is a sense in which the Presbyterians from the South could not have given their allegiance and encouragement to the Federal government, even if they had desired to do so. They were technically citizens of another nation, at least in their own eyes, and they thus considered approval of the Spring proposals tantamount to treason. By way of a theoretical answer to the resolutions, they chose to argue that the Philadelphia Assembly had made a *political* deliverance, over which it—as a *spiritual* assemblage—had no proper authority. This was a view which was shared by a minority among the Northern commissioners at the Assembly, including the noted theologian, Dr. Charles Hodge of Princeton.

By way of a practical answer, though, their only possible response was to organize a separate church within the bounds of the Confederate States. During the summer of 1861, one Southern presbytery after another withdrew from the jurisdiction of the Presbyterian Church in the U.S.A., until eventually all forty-seven had withdrawn. In each case the presbytery gave the unconstitutional character of the Gardiner Spring Resolutions as the reason for its decision. In August, a number of the withdrawing presbyteries were represented at a convention held in Atlanta for the purpose of laying plans for the organization of the Presbyterian Church in the Confederate States of America.

Pursuant to the convention's plan, the commissioners from the forty-seven presbyteries gathered in Augusta on December 4, 1861 for the first meeting of the new General Assembly. Benjamin M. Palmer, pastor of the First Presbyterian Church of New Orleans, was generally acknowledged to be one of the two most important leaders of the new assembly. Palmer preached the opening sermon on the subject "The Headship of Christ Over the Church," and soon thereafter was elected moderator of the newly constituted body.

The other man of great significance in the first General Assembly was James Henley Thornwell, Professor of Theology at Columbia Theological Seminary. One of the early actions of the Assembly was to name Thornwell to chair a committee charged with the responsibility of drafting "An Address to All the Churches of Jesus Christ Throughout the Earth," explaining why the new denomination had withdrawn from the Presbyterian Church U.S.A., and setting forth some of the principles for which the new body would stand.

Most of the reasons given for the separation, such as the problem of slavery, the existence of the new Confederate nation, and the unconstitutional character of the Spring resolutions, were practical matters that would have been entirely predictable to any thoughtful observer. Undergirding the whole, however, were two rather substantial differences in theory, which were to serve for a good many years thereafter as important clues to the character of the denomination which had just come into being.

One of these issues, underscored quite directly by the choice of Thornwell to chair the committee which drafted the "Address," was the question of how best to organize the church for its mission. As we shall see presently, Thornwell had been involved in a long and sometimes heated controversy in previous years over whether the church should *have* missionary agencies, or whether it *was itself* supposed to be such an instrument of mission in its entirety.

The other issue, in which the presence of Thornwell is equally significant, was the matter of the "spirituality" of the church. In the years leading up to the war, it had been the conventional wisdom of Southern Presbyterians—with Thornwell again as their most articulate spokesman—that their Northern brethren were drifting toward apostasy by intermingling religion and politics. Most particularly, of course, they perceived this drift taking place with regard to slavery and the knotty complex of issues which surrounded it. The church, the Southerners contended, is empowered to express itself only in those areas which are manifestly "spiritual." This concept of the "spirituality of the church" is an idea which E. T. Thompson has described as "a distinctive doctrine

of the Presbyterian Church in the United States." It persisted in Southern Presbyterianism throughout the time of Civil War and Reconstruction, and it persists in some quarters right down to the present day.
Though many today would argue, with no little evidence on their side,
that this runs contrary to earlier phases of our Reformed heritage, such
as the developments in Calvin's Geneva or Puritan England, we cannot
deny that this idea emerged from the debates over slavery to play an
important role in the subsequent development of our denomination.

When the first General Assembly had ended, our new denomination found itself born to a ministry in the midst of anguish and failure.
The story of the Southern trauma over the next four years is punctuated
by the efforts of Presbyterian pastors and laypeople to encourage the
representatives of their Lost Cause, and to bind up the spiritual wounds
brought on by the inevitable defeat. The occasional bright moments of
those days, such as the remarkable revivals which occurred among the
Confederate troops in 1863 and 1864, are vastly overshadowed by the
agony of the times.

Reconstruction and Renewal

The close of hostilities in 1865 did not signal an end to the tribula-
tion of the church. The name was changed soon enough—P.C.C.S.A.
became P.C.U.S. almost at once—but the scars of the horrible conflict
persisted. Northern Presbyterians offered ecclesiastical reunion upon
terms of repentance. Southern Presbyterians quickly and totally rejected
the offer. In retrospect, both the offer and the refusal seem sadly lacking
in charity; feelings still ran far too high. The two churches were destined
to remain apart for a long time to come.

In many respects, the fortunes of the Southern church were as low
as those of the entire region. Some congregations had lost their meeting
places to the ravages of war. Others had suffered even more seriously,
losing irreplaceable pastoral and lay leadership among the casualties.
Almost without exception, the financial resources of the churches were
gone. One Alabama congregation watched a deacons' fund of several
hundred Confederate dollars reduced in a moment to half of a one-dollar
gold piece.

Nevertheless, there were some elements of encouragement in the
Southern story, even in those earliest days. The war and post-war years

witnessed the incorporation of several smaller Presbyterian bodies into the Presbyterian Church in the United States. Fifteen years after its organization, the denomination had grown by fifteen thousand members, largely through the reception of such smaller groups as the Independent Presbyterian Church (1863), the United Synod of the South (New School) (1864), the Presbytery of Patapsco (1867), the Alabama Presbytery of the Associate Reformed Church (1867), a portion of the Synod of Kentucky (1870), and a portion of the Synod of Missouri (1874).

This modest growth was attended by an expanding sense of mission, both at home and abroad. In its first "Address to All the Churches" the Southern Presbyterian communion had committed itself to being a missionary church. Now, the privations of the Reconstruction period notwithstanding, it began to make good on that commitment. J. Leighton Wilson, a former missionary to Africa, provided the needed administrative skills for an active program of home and foreign missions. Southern Presbyterian missionaries were at work in China, Italy, Colombia, Brazil, Mexico, and Greece within a decade after the close of the Civil War. On the home front, missionaries worked not only in unchurched areas of the southwestern frontier, but among the former slaves whose lives had been so radically changed by the coming of emancipation. In 1877, a school for the training of black pastors was organized in Tuscaloosa, which was later to become Stillman College.

In addition to this great missionary emphasis, higher education also emerged as one of the major concerns of the post-Civil War church. At the time of the separation in 1861, several significant Presbyterian colleges, such as Hampden-Sydney, Centre, Davidson, and Queens had fallen under the care of the new denomination. In addition, two seminaries, Columbia in South Carolina and Union in Virginia, were also within its bounds. In the years following the war, other colleges, such as King (1867), Arkansas (1872), Southwestern (consolidated from other institutions in 1875), and Presbyterian (1880) came into existence. Eventually the denomination boasted more than two dozen junior and senior colleges, four seminaries, and a professional school of Christian education.

The passage of years between the birth of our denomination and today have witnessed growth and development in many other areas of our experience. Of particular interest to our study are developments in the areas of theological activity, ecumenical affairs, and church organization.

Theological Development

The theological stance of the Southern Presbyterian Church at the time of its establishment was unquestionably Calvinist. Except for certain distinctive points of emphasis, such as the idea of the spirituality of the church, which both emerged from and shaped our historical experience, our theological life has faithfully reproduced the major lineaments of the Reformed heritage. From time to time, however, new ideas have excited a measure of ferment and debate within the denomination.

In the latter decades of the nineteenth century, for example, the evolution controversy produced considerable conflict among Southern Presbyterians. Professor James Woodrow of Columbia Seminary (the uncle of President Woodrow Wilson), was the focal figure in a debate which occupied the attention of the church for better than a decade. Woodrow was eventually compelled to resign his position at Columbia, and the General Assembly delivered itself of a statement condemning the theory of evolution. Ironically, though, the lasting result of the controversy may well have been the emergence of a spirit of latitude and tolerance within the church.

At first, the Presbyterian Church, U.S., seems to have handled the Westminster Confession of Faith as though it were sacrosanct and unalterable—an attitude which surely would have puzzled its original authors! It took years of debate and discussion before the General Assembly made its first amendment to the Confession in 1886, by eliminating the statement in the original document which prohibited marriage to the sibling of a deceased spouse. After that minor change, there were no further alterations for more than fifty years. Finally, in 1939, verbal changes were made in eleven different paragraphs of the Confession, such as the instance in which the original document referred to the Roman Pope as the "Antichrist" and the Roman churches as "Synagogues of Satan." In 1942 two new chapters were added, one on "The Holy Spirit" and the other on "The Gospel," in order to enhance the scope of the Confession's theological system. Basically, though, the original document has provided the substance of the theological position of our denomination.

In recent years, we have given serious consideration to the possibility of broadening that confessional basis. In 1969 the General Assembly appointed a committee with the task of submitting to the church a proposed book of confessions, to include historical representations of the Reformed heritage as well as a statement of faith in contemporary language. The committee made its report to the 1976 General Assembly, offering a proposed collection which added seven other statements of faith to the Westminster Confession and Catechisms. These were: the Nicene Creed, the Apostles' Creed, the Geneva Catechism, the Scots Confession, the Heidelberg Catechism, the Theological Declaration of Barmen, and the contemporary Declaration of Faith, which had been drafted by the committee itself. The 1976 Assembly approved the proposed book by a large margin, and sent it down to the presbyteries for their advice and consent. For a variety of reasons, it failed to receive the necessary three-fourths majority of the presbyteries needed to secure its adoption. Thus the Westminster Confession and Catechisms continue presently as the only theological standard for our denomination.

Even most of those who opposed this particular book of confessions agree with its supporters, though, that the process of reflection, study, and debate which the recent confessional activity provided was altogether helpful to our denomination. Many feel that our faithfulness to the dynamic spirit of Protestantism implies that we will continue this process of making and remaking our confession, and that eventually we will move toward the adoption of the sort of book of confessions which was recently under consideration.

Ecumenical Relationships

In the "Address to the Churches of Jesus Christ Throughout the World," issued by the first General Assembly in 1861, these words occur: "We offer you the right hand of fellowship. . . . We greet you in the ties of Christian brotherhood. We desire to cultivate peace and charity with our fellow Christians throughout the world." Sad to say, the bitter experience of the war and Reconstruction years dampened the enthusiasm with which the hand of fellowship was extended in some directions. Although friendly relations came early with the Scottish church and some of the continental churches in the Reformed tradition, it was not until 1882 that fraternal relations were established with the Presbyterian Church in the United States of America. This step, however, gave a real ring of authenticity to an earlier decision, made with some misgivings in 1876, to become a participant in the organization known as the World Alliance of Reformed Churches. This alliance, now over a century old, is comprised of nearly all of the churches in the Reformed tradition, and we can be proud that our denomination was a charter participant.

Eventually the ties of cooperation and comradeship were extended beyond the Reformed family. In 1912, our denomination committed itself, again not without misgivings, to membership in the Federal Council of Churches of Christ in America. Although there was a decade during which our membership in that organization was suspended (1931–41), our reentry was accomplished in time for participation in the transformation of that body into the National Council of Churches in 1950. The Presbyterian Church, U.S., is also a member of the World Council of Churches, which includes Christian groups from a myriad of traditions throughout the world. In 1966 our denomination became a full participant in an organization known as the Consultation on Church Union, which has as its major concern the facilitation of united efforts on the part of several major American denominations, including Methodists, Episcopalians, Lutherans, and Baptists, as well as Presbyterians.

One element of persistent concern for many within our denomination throughout its century of existence has been the prospect for reunion with the body from which we were divided by the Civil War. Through the years there have been several serious attempts to draw the two denominations back together. A major effort was concluded unsuccessfully in 1954, when the Presbyterian Church U.S.A. and the United Presbyterian Church merged to form the United Presbyterian Church in the United States of America. Southern Presbyterians decided not to join at that juncture. At this writing, though, yet another such effort is under way, and will soon be subject to the decision of the two denominations.

Organization for the Church's Mission

As we have mentioned before, when the General Assembly of the Presbyterian Church in the Confederate States of America was organized in 1861, one of the issues of conflict which was mentioned by the newly organized body in its "Address to All the Churches" was the matter of how a church should organize itself for its mission. For a number of years before the division, the Presbyterian Church in the U.S.A. had operated through denominational boards, which were created to perform specific tasks, such as home missions or publication, in the name of the whole General Assembly. Opponents of this system, such as James Henley Thornwell, argued that such a system was unscriptural and that these agencies tended to operate with some independence from the wishes and guidance of the church itself. A great debate on the subject took place between Dr. Thornwell and Dr. Hodge of Princeton at the General Assembly in 1860, with Hodge carrying the day by a lopsided margin of about five to one.

When the Presbyterian Church C.S.A. was formed, however, there was no Hodge to oppose the Thornwell point of view, and it must have seemed a foregone conclusion from the outset that there would be no boards in the new church. Instead, there were executive committees which were to do their work under rather specific instructions from the General Assembly. The first Assembly created four of these committees: Foreign Missions, Home Missions, Publication, and Christian Education. Other committees came into existence in later years, but in due time they were combined with one of the four named above. The duties of the four were substantially enlarged as years went by, and slight changes were made in the names of some of them.

Basically, though, these four agencies served the needs of the denomination from 1861 until 1949. During those eighty-eight years, the distinction between executive committees and boards largely disappeared. Thus, the General Assembly of 1949 discontinued the use of the term "executive committee" and returned to the name "board" which had been abandoned in 1861. There was also a realignment of functions among the boards, and the official addition of two others—the Board of Women's Work and the Board of Annuities and Relief—as the restructuring took place. The headquarters of the various boards were in different major cities—Atlanta, Nashville, and Richmond—and each operated in relative independence from the others. Nevertheless, this new system of organization provided effective specialized leadership and resources for the denomination in a period of considerable growth and development.

Eventually, though, it seemed apparent to many within the life of the Presbyterian Church, U.S., that the physical and functional separation of the various boards and agencies frequently led to duplication of effort and difficulty of communication, both with one another and with the church at large. With this in mind, the General Assembly began planning in 1969 for a thorough restructuring of the church's organization. The committee which was assigned the task of establishing a new model reported to the Assembly in 1972, and soon thereafter our present system of organization at the denominational level was put into effect.

The General Assembly Mission Board

The key ingredient in our present system is a central coordinating body, drawn from all quarters of our church's life, known as the General Assembly Mission Board. There are fifty-seven members of the Mission Board, of whom forty (half clergy and half lay) are regional representatives, fourteen are nominated by the Assembly's nominating committee to insure adequate representatives for minority groups, and three are executive officers. Each person on the Mission Board is elected for a three-year term, and it is possible to serve for two terms only. It is intended that ministers and laypeople representing the whole spectrum of interest and viewpoint in the denomination be chosen to serve on this board.

The General Assembly Mission Board is responsible to the General Assembly itself for the accomplishment of two basic tasks. The first of these is the implementation of the program which the Assembly has chosen, and the second is the maintenance of the means of communication and assistance within the denomination. The "official" terms for these responsibilities, respectively, are the Program System and the Court Partnership System.

For the accomplishment of these tasks, the Mission Board is organized into an administrative committee and five functional divisions. Each of these groups has a professional staff available to it, with offices in the Presbyterian Center in Atlanta. Like the members of the board themselves, the primary staff members are also elected for limited terms of service. The five functional divisions are entitled Central Support Services, Corporate and Social Mission, Court Partnership Services, International Mission, and National Mission. It will be a good thing for us to be acquainted with the tasks of each:

The Division of Central Support Services is responsible for administrative activities of the General Assembly, such as the financial and records management activities of our organization. It is also responsible for the practical aspects of publication and distribution of denominational materials, including the activities of the John Knox Press, which published the book you are reading. The relationship between our denomination and the various communications media is under the oversight of this division as well.

The Division of Corporate and Social Mission is designated as the agency of the Mission Board which maintains our sensitivity and witness in the areas of ecumenical and public affairs. Through it, we are kept in touch with the issues and activities abroad in the larger Christian community, and we are enabled to express our concerns for justice and compassion in political and social affairs.

The Division of Court Partnership Services is assigned the task of maintaining the lines of communication between and among the General Assembly and the other judicatories of our denomination, such as synods, presbyteries, and local congregations. The stewardship and budgeting process is a part of the responsibility of this division, as is the enterprise of developing the professional leadership for our church.

The Division of International Mission continues the historic concern of our denomination for the progress of the witness to the gospel throughout the world. Working as partners with the indigenous Christian communities in such places as Taiwan, Korea, Indonesia, Japan, Mexico, Haiti, and Zaire, representatives of our church provide necessary services for the fulfillment of the mission of the universal church. This division also has present responsibility for our participation in the programs directed toward the alleviation of world hunger.

The Division of National Mission has oversight of the denominational aspects of the task of Christian Education, such as curriculum and teacher development. It is also responsible for our programs of evangelism and new church development, and for liaison with various Assembly-operated institutions such as Montreat, Stillman College, and the

Presbyterian School of Christian Education. The Offices of Women's Work and Chaplains and Military Personnel are also placed in this division.

A major portion of the activity of the General Assembly is conducted through these various divisions of the General Assembly Mission Board. The task of the board and its professional staff is not to create new policies or priorities, but to interpret and implement the priorities and policies established by the General Assembly itself. In order to provide a means of assessing this work, the Assembly has constituted an independent Office of Review and Evaluation, responsible directly to the Assembly itself, which is charged with the task of presenting annual evaluations of the activities of the Mission Board and its staff.

Other General Assembly Agencies

In addition to the various aspects of the program and court partnership systems which we have summarized heretofore, there are other activities and agencies of the General Assembly which ought to be recognized by knowledgeable Presbyterians. There is, for example, the Board of Annuities and Relief, which exists within the Assembly's structure with a measure of independence, in order to provide the various "fringe" benefits for ministers and lay employees of the church, such as hospitalization and life insurance, retirement benefits, and the like. There is also the Presbyterian Foundation, which is charged with the responsibility of managing and investing bequests, trust funds and endowments which come to the denomination from members and friends.

Another area of activity which deserves mention is the collection of offices, councils and committees, both temporary and permanent, which are directly related to the Assembly itself, rather than to its Mission Board, because of their lack of connection with the year-by-year program planning of the church. In one way or another, each of these serves a monitoring function. The Office of Review and Evaluation, mentioned above, is one such agency. Others include the Office of the Stated Clerk, which interprets and applies the constitution of the church; the Committees on Women's Concerns and Church and Race, which seek to assure justice in these areas of the church's life; the Committee on Presbyterian and Reformed History, which attends to the archival and historical activities of the church; and the Council on Theology and Culture, which assists the church in its effort to interpret the faith in the light of contemporary life. All of these "non-program" agencies are related to the Assembly through its Committee on Assembly Operations, which oversees their activities and develops the plans for the annual meetings of the General Assembly itself.

The Purpose of the General Assembly

The question is sometimes asked, "Why do all these diverse (and sometimes confusing) institutional structures exist?" Some even wonder if we have not created a situation in which these divisions, offices, and agencies which we have been discussing actually *become* the Presbyterian Church in the United States, leaving all of us in the local churches out in the cold.

The answer, of course, is that all these various organs are designed to be the *servants* of the church, in helping us to identify our mission emphases and move toward the achievement of our goals in those areas. The genius of the system, as we have been observing throughout our study, is that there is no such thing as a Pope or a hierarchical succession of power in the Presbyterian Church.

Chances are that any member of the Presbyterian Church in the United States who reads this book will know someone personally who either serves on the General Assembly Mission Board, or works in one of the varied agencies of the Assembly, or has been a participant in one or more of the meetings of the Assembly itself. There is no better way of being reminded of the nature of our involvement in the affairs of the church than to reflect upon the ways in which we are personally connected with its decisions and activities.

The Mission Board and its staff intend to be our representatives in continuing the witness of all of us who are involved in the 880,000-member Presbyterian Church in the United States—in our own congregations, in the geographical boundaries of our denomination, and in the life of the world.

Chapter Nine

OTHER
PRESBYTERIAN BODIES

In the preceding chapters we have traced what might be called the genealogy of our own Presbyterian heritage in Europe and America. There are other important Presbyterian groups, not only in this country, but also in other lands which have not yet been mentioned in our narrative. Even a short history of Presbyterianism such as this is not complete without at least a few comments concerning some of these churches.

In the United States

There are well over a dozen Presbyterian and Reformed denominations in the United States, with a total membership of over four million. Almost three and a half million of these are found in the two churches upon which we have focussed our attention in the previous chapters. The others are scattered among the several bodies, both large and small, which are described in the following paragraphs.

The Associate Reformed Presbyterian Church (General Synod). The history of the Associate Reformed Presbyterian Church (which is usually identified by its initials in informal conversation) goes back to 1733, when Ebenezer Erskine withdrew from the Church of Scotland and organized the Associate Presbytery. In America, Erskine's followers were originally a part of the Covenanter group calling itself the Associate

Reformed Church, which had its two main concentrations of strength in Pennsylvania and the South. In the early 1820s the Southern portion of the group withdrew to form the Associate Reformed Synod of the South. When the United Presbyterian Church was organized in 1858 as a union of several strands of the Scottish Covenanter and Seceder traditions, this Southern synod did not join.

The A.R.P. church uses the Westminster Confession and Catechisms as its doctrinal standards. Until recently, one of its most distinctive "family" characteristics was the use of the Psalms as the only appropriate materials for singing in public worship. The primary concentrations of A.R.P. churches are in the Carolinas, Georgia, and Tennessee. Its educational center is Erskine College and Erskine Theological Seminary in Due West, South Carolina. In the late 1970s, the membership was just over 31,000.

The Cumberland Presbyterian Church. As we have seen, the Cumberland Church had its origins in the great revivals that swept over Kentucky and Tennessee in the early part of the nineteenth century. A dispute arose among frontier Presbyterians concerning the best way to respond to the religious needs of their area. Some advocated lowering the academic standards for ordination to the ministry, in order to provide leadership for the scores of people who were being converted through the revivals. Generally speaking, these disputants also advocated a more Arminian view of theology, evoked in part by their observation of the importance of the human will in revival activity.

This dispute resulted in the organization of the Cumberland Presbyterian Church in 1810. The new church advocated the ordination of spiritually minded men who had preaching gifts, whether or not they had the usual theological education. The Cumberland Church also made some modifications to the Westminster Confession, in order to eliminate what some of its members considered to be a fatalistic view of human salvation.

By the end of the nineteenth century, the Cumberland Church had almost 200,000 members. In 1906, as we have mentioned earlier, a reunion was effected between the Cumberland Church and the Presbyterian Church U.S.A. About a third of the Cumberland membership was unwilling to make the merger, however, so their denomination remained in existence, though substantially smaller than before. In the late 1970s, its membership was over 94,000. Its main areas of strength are the Southern states, especially Kentucky and Tennessee. It sponsors Bethel College and Cumberland Theological Seminary, both in Tennessee.

There is also a Second Cumberland Presbyterian Church in the United States, comprised of black churches of Cumberland background which were placed under a separate administration in 1869. In the 1970s, this church reported a membership of just over six thousand.

The Reformed Church in America. In 1867, the Dutch Reformed Church, largely the product of Dutch colonization in New York, changed its name to the Reformed Church in America. Despite the lack of the term "presbyterian" in its name, the R.C.A. is very much a part of the Presbyterian family. Its doctrinal standards are the Belgic Confession, the Heidelberg Catechism, and the Canons of the Synod of Dort, all of which are thoroughly Calvinistic in tone.

In the 1960s, our denomination entered serious negotiations with the Reformed Church in America, with an eye toward the eventual union of the two denominations. A combination of circumstances prevented the marriage, but at least the conversations served to establish a warm fraternal relationship between the two churches. The geographical concentrations of the R.C.A. are the New York-New Jersey area and the state of Michigan. In the late 1970s, the membership of this church was over 213,000.

The Christian Reformed Church. The Christian Reformed Church withdrew from the Dutch Reformed Church, because of a more conservative attitude on several matters of doctrine and church discipline. It continues to be known today for a very intense and rigid adherence to Calvinistic doctrine. Most of its membership, which numbered over 280,000 in the late 1970s, is located in the state of Michigan.

The Orthodox Presbyterian Church. A new Presbyterian denomination was organized in 1936, as a part of a movement out of the Presbyterian Church U.S.A. led by Professor J. Gresham Machen of Princeton Theological Seminary. Originally called the Presbyterian Church in America, this group changed its name to the Orthodox

Presbyterian Church in 1938. The O.P.C. has laid special emphasis upon certain doctrinal opinions, such as the inerrancy of Scripture, at the same time that it adheres to the Westminster Confession and Catechisms as its doctrinal standards. In the 1970s it reported a membership of almost 15,000 members.

The Bible Presbyterian Church. The Bible Presbyterian Church withdrew from the Orthodox Presbyterian Church in 1938, after a dispute which centered on abstinence from the use of alcoholic beverages and the necessity of believing in the premillennial return of Christ. The Bible Church amended the Westminster Confession so that it would reflect this premillennial theology. Under the initial leadership of Dr. Carl McIntire, this church has had a continued history of controversy and division. There were about 8,000 members of the Bible Presbyterian Church in the 1970s.

The Reformed Presbyterian Church of North America. Another of the descendents of the Scottish Covenanter lineage, the Reformed Presbyterian Church of North America has been remarkable among American Presbyterian groups for its position with regard to secular authority. The members of this church are reluctant to participate in the public affairs of a nation which does not give specific constitutional recognition to God as the source of all power, Christ as the ruler of nations, the Bible as the supreme guide of life, and Christianity as the one true religion. Up until 1964, the denomination barred its members from voting or otherwise participating in civic affairs. Most of the five thousand members live in Pennsylvania, where the denomination operates Geneva College.

The Reformed Presbyterian Church, Evangelical Synod. This church was organized in 1965 by a merger of two intensely conservative groups, one of which represented the same non-political tradition mentioned above. The other party to the union was a group which had split from the Orthodox and Bible Churches some years before. The Reformed Presbyterian Church, Evangelical Synod, is intensely conservative, and requires a very strict adherence to the Westminster Confession and Catechisms. The church operates Covenant College in Lookout Mountain, Tennessee, and Covenant Theological Seminary in St. Louis.

The membership of the group in the late 1970s was almost 24,000.

The Presbyterian Church in America. One of the newer American denominations is the group which withdrew from the Presbyterian Church in the United States in late 1973 over a variety of social and doctrinal issues. The group originally took the name "National Presbyterian Church," but changed at its second General Assembly to the title "Presbyterian Church in America." The denomination advocates the view of the inerrancy of Scripture, and a rather rigid adherance to the original doctrinal statements of the Westminster Assembly. In social matters the P.C.A. claims to continue the tradition of the spirituality of the church. At the time of its separation from the Presbyterian Church in the United States, this church claimed about ninety thousand members, a great many of whom are in Alabama and Mississippi.

International Presbyterianism

The Presbyterian Church in Canada. Presbyterians from Scotland laid the foundations for the Presbyterian Church in Canada, and in many ways the early history of the Canadian church was a mirror of the various difficulties and divisions of the Scottish church. In 1875 the various groups were brought together into one national church. Fifty years later, when the United Church of Canada was formed by the merger of the Congregational, Methodist, and Presbyterian churches, a sizable minority of Canadian Presbyterians refused to participate in the merger, and continued to carry on their separate tradition. In 1975 the Canadian Presbyterian Church numbered about 175,000 members. The United Church of Canada, which is itself a member of the World Alliance of Reformed Churches, has a membership of over a million.

The Presbyterian Church of Australia. The Australian Presbyterian Church is also largely of Scottish origins, and has also reflected the various divisions and reunions of the Scottish church. In 1901, the year after the six states of the continent had come together to form the Commonwealth of Australia, the Presbyterians of the states convened to form a national church. Because of the vastness of the continent and the relative sparseness of the population, each of the state Presbyterian organizations continues to maintain a considerable degree of autonomy. In the early 1970s, the communicant membership of the denomination was just over 150,000.

The Presbyterian Church of New Zealand. The origins and subsequent history of the Presbyterian Church in New Zealand are largely parallel to the experience of the Australian church. In 1901 various Presbyterian groups came together and formed a united denomination, which is known for its strong emphasis upon academic activity. There were nearly 100,000 communicant members of this church in the early 1970s.

Presbyterian Churches of Africa. Many of the emerging nations on the continent of Africa boast young and vigorous national churches, brought into being through the missionary efforts of Presbyterians from the United States and Europe, but now full partners in the church's mission with those older groups. Of special interest to the members of the Presbyterian Church in the United States is the Presbyterian Church in the Republic of Zaire (formerly Congo), which has been an area of our fraternal concern for more than a century. That church now has a baptized membership of almost 150,000. There are also large and strong Presbyterian communities in such African nations as Malawi (265,000), Cameroon (70,000), Kenya (62,000), and Ghana (90,000).

In southern Africa, there is a vigorous Presbyterian tradition, both among blacks and whites. Both the Scottish and Dutch Reformed churches were major factors in the original colonial settlement of that area, and the communicant membership of the multiple offspring of those churches in southern Africa is well over a million. It has been encouraging in recent years to see some effort for the alleviation of the *apartheid* policies of the region emerging from a prophetic minority within the Reformed community there.

Presbyterian Churches in Asia and Latin America. Strong native churches have also emerged in some areas of the world that are largely dominated by other religious traditions. In Asia, for example, there are strong Presbyterian communities in Korea, Japan, and Taiwan, all of which have strong fraternal ties to the Presbyterian Church in the United States. The church in Korea has exhibited special vigor in recent years. Perhaps the largest Presbyterian congregation in the world is located in the city of Seoul.

In Latin America, small but vigorous Presbyterian groups exist in several nations, despite the predominance of Roman Catholicism there.

Mexico and Brazil, in particular, have vital churches, both of which have roots in the missionary activity of the Presbyterian Church in the United States.

Other Presbyterian Churches in Europe. In previous chapters we traced the history of those Presbyterian and Reformed communions in Europe which made large contributions to the growth of American Presbyterianism. There are other groups of Presbyterians in Europe, however, which have not been mentioned in detail. Most of them are called Reformed churches, but they are Calvinist in doctrine and presbyterian in polity. There are, of course, strong churches in Germany and Switzerland, and there is even activity behind the Iron Curtain in such places as Hungary, Poland, Rumania, and Yugoslavia. All of these churches have fellowship with the larger world community through the organization known as the World Alliance of Reformed Churches.

The World Alliance. Since the Reformation, Presbyterians have spread through migration and missionary labor to all parts of the world, and Presbyterianism has become a "catholic" movement, in the best sense of that term. In 1877, at the city of Edinburgh, the members of this world Presbyterian family came together for the first time for a sort of reunion. The organization which emerged from that first gathering bore the title "The Alliance of Reformed Churches Throughout the World Holding the Presbyterian Order."

This organization, now a century old, has served to bear witness to the values of our heritage and to render special assistance to various member churches. In 1970, at a meeting in Nairobi, Kenya, the Alliance merged with the Council of Congregational Churches, forming the World Alliance of Reformed Churches (Presbyterian and Congregational). It is impossible to say precisely how many churches or how many Christians are encompassed in this worldwide community, and there is a sense in which such figures do not really matter after all.

The great significance of the World Alliance is the fact that here people from every corner of the earth meet to share a common heritage and a common commitment to God's purposes in the future of our world.

Chapter Ten

BASIC
PRESBYTERIAN BELIEFS

Our Confessional Tradition

If we consider the diversity of attitudes and experiences which we have encountered in our brief survey of the Presbyterian story, it might seem to be a risky thing to try to say "what Presbyterians believe," because there have been notable differences of opinion among those who share our heritage. The risk is not quite as great as it might seem, however, since ours is a tradition which has left landmarks along the way.

We are known as a "confessional" church. This means, as we have already seen, that we have undertaken in various times and situations to *confess* or state our beliefs in systematic form for the rest of the world to see. From Geneva, from France, from the Netherlands, from Scotland, from Puritan England, from twentieth century America—from several dozen specific sets of circumstances all told—the Reformed tradition has produced its statements of faith.

In some of these instances, the church has confessed as an embattled minority, ready to draft its signature in blood, if need be. In others, the church has spoken from a position of strength, ready to dictate a guidebook of faith by which an entire nation should live. Sometimes the statements have been made in humility, with a plea for other Christians to offer biblical correctives, where necessary. In other cases, the statements have been made with great confidence—not to say arrogance—upon the presumption that the tradition has already proven its fidelity to Scripture and Christian experience.

In almost every case, though, the writers have intended to state cogently the basic and necessary principles of Christianity as they have discovered them in Scripture. Obviously they had assistance in the confessional process from other sources. They listened to earlier confessions; they listened to the great theologians of the church; they listened, most of all, for the guidance of the Holy Spirit as they worked.

There is a refreshing variety in the finished products of their efforts. To some extent, the confessions themselves are a memory-book of rhetorical style and theological fashion. When all is said and done, however, there is a certain consistency to the main features of Reformed confessions. Time and again, the same points of emphasis recur. As we conclude this survey of our heritage, these are the basic features of "Presbyterian" belief which ought to be identified—not because we are the only ones who have believed these things, but because we have found them to be somehow central to our understanding of the faith. In this chapter it is our purpose to consider several of these basic emphases.

The Sovereignty of God

We have observed in an earlier chapter that the concept of the sovereignty of God is the central sun around which everything else in our doctrinal system seems to revolve. When we say that God is "sovereign," we mean that he is in absolute control of the universe, and that he is absolutely independent of any other power or will. When we try to amplify or explain this idea of sovereignty, we sometimes find ourselves reduced to the repetition of superlatives. God is the most, the best, the greatest—in every area of our comprehension.

Many of our Reformed confessions have depended upon this mode of expression in speaking about God. The Larger Catechism of Westminster, for example, states its definition of God as the One who is "in and of Himself infinite in being, glory, blessedness, and perfection; all-sufficient, eternal, unchangeable, incomprehensible, everywhere present, almighty, knowing all things, most wise, most holy, most just, most merciful and gracious, long-suffering, and abundant in goodness and truth." In this and other similar statements, we have affirmed the idea that we cannot overestimate the perfection of God.

Such lists of virtues do not, however, represent the real essential core of our understanding of God. For one thing, we soon learn that we are over our depth when we try to comprehend the magnificence of God in frail and fallible words. Many of our adjectives of praise are simply images of human qualities magnified to their nth degree, and fail to do justice to our belief in God as one who is not limited to the traits of creatureliness.

More significantly, though, we recognize that our representations of God simply in terms of superlative characteristics can distract us from the essential Reformed belief that God is known to us primarily in terms of his *action* rather than in terms of his *perfection*. We are not so much concerned with the vision of God (as one finds emphasized in other Christian traditions) as we are with our experience of his purposeful activity in our lives and in the life of the world. Simply put, we believe that we know God more certainly in his deeds than we do in his attributes.

The doctrine of the sovereignty of God means, furthermore, that we know the actions of God to be intentional, and directed toward the accomplishment of his purposes in his creation. Our Reformed forebears spent much time in stressing and explaining the importance of what they called the "decrees" of God. By this they intended to underscore the precise and purposeful involvement of God in all our affairs. Wrote the Westminster divines, "God from all eternity did by the most wise and holy counsel of his own will freely and unchangeably ordain whatsoever comes to pass." Things happen because God *means* for them to happen; all that comes in life is grounded in his will and intention.

It is not too much to say that this conception of God is determinative for our whole understanding of religion. If we begin with the affirmation that God is in control of the world in which we live, and if we remind ourselves that he is not only the Creator of this world, but its Redeemer and Sanctifier as well, then we see that everything else that we know—about ourselves and the world around us—is never far removed from this one essential which we affirm.

This doctrine of the sovereignty of God has been of great consolation to many Presbyterians who have lived in times like those through which our world has been passing in recent years. If we did not believe that the Lord God omnipotent actually reigns, we might be distracted or discouraged by the immediate perils of modern life. Believing this, though, we have access to a great source of comfort and strength "for the living of these days."

Predestination—God's Eternal Plan

In the Reformed tradition, one of the most important and distinctive corollaries of this central doctrine of the sovereignty of God is the idea of predestination. In the technical, theological sense, the term "predestination" is concerned primarily with those plans and purposes of God which relate to our eternal destiny as his creatures. In popular usage, however, the word has come to be understood as a comprehensive view of God's plan for his creation and everything in it.

It is likely that no one can have had sufficient interest to read this far in this particular book without also being well aware of the oft-heard exclamation, *"Presbyterians* believe in *predestination!"* And most who have heard that statement remember it as something of an allegation, as though the last word were some sort of congenital, if not contagious, disease. In fact, predestination all too often turns out to be the "bad rap" which is identified as the one serious shortcoming of our inheritance. Charles Williams, the British lay-theologian, once wrote: "A new insight is quite sound when a master uses it, cheapens as it becomes popular, and is unendurable when it is merely fashionable. So Augustine's predestination was safe with him, comprehensible in Calvin, tiresome in the English Puritans, and quite horrible in the Scottish presbyteries."

Perhaps this criticism is accurate, but unfair. In any event, we should not surrender too easily to the notion that predestination is simply a stigma that we must bear. In plainest terms, the nucleus of this doctrine is the simple fact, witnessed in common experience as well as in the biblical narrative, that God calls human beings (or at least some humans) to a special relationship and destiny, and that humanity (or, again, at least some parts of it) seems to respond in devotion to God and in commitment to his will for their lives. If one asks why or how God chooses, the only answer we have found to be adequate is an affirmation of the sheer mystery of it all: He chooses to choose "of his mere good pleasure," without any reference to considerations that we might like to raise on our own behalf.

To say that a person is numbered among God's elect, therefore, is to say nothing whatsoever about the qualifications or achievements of that person; it is simply to say something about the decision of a sovereign God. It is not a badge of privilege for that person, but an indication that he or she is called and committed to service in God's behalf.

The question has frequently been raised about the viability of any notion of human freedom if one holds seriously to the idea of predestination. Theologians of the Reformed tradition have faced this paradox of predestination and free will, and have generally concluded that the freedom of the will, though authentic and unmistakable as far as human perception and experience is concerned, is nonetheless limited by our nature as creatures. We are subjects of God's sovereign will whether we know it or not.

A more serious question, at least from the theological point of view, is one which has been the topic of considerable debate *within* the Reformed community in recent generations. It is the matter of the logical derivation of our basic doctrine of election, which has come to be known by the name "double predestination." Double predestination is the conviction that if God actively chooses some people, he therefore must choose not to choose some others. Some of our Reformed confessions make this presumption quite directly. The Westminster Confession, for example, plainly asserts: "The rest of mankind, God was pleased, according to the unsearchable counsel of his own will, whereby he extendeth or withholdeth mercy as he pleaseth, for the glory of his sovereign power over his creatures, to pass by, and to ordain them to dishonor and wrath for their sin, to the praise of his glorious justice."

Many Reformed Christians, while acknowledging the logical consistency of such a view and denying the validity of the opposite extreme which asserts that all will be saved (sometimes called universalism), nevertheless have great difficulty with the view that God would create some human beings for the eventual purpose of damning them. They take comfort from the last paragraph of the Confession's chapter on the subject, which asserts that predestination is a "high mystery" which must be handled with "special prudence and care."

At its worst, the doctrine of predestination has been a source of censorious superiority, by which people have wrought judgment upon the lives of their neighbors. At its best, however, it has been a source of great comfort for those who have sought to align their lives with the plan of God. It has been a mark of God's call to duty, providing a profound warrant for active and selfless involvement in the life of the world which God has both created and sustained.

The Nature of Humanity

Another corollary of the remarkable emphasis which our tradition has placed upon the sovereignty of God is the way in which we have been inclined to view human nature and our status in life as God's creatures. There are two aspects of this area of Reformed doctrine which need to be held in balance.

The first grows from the very positive affirmation that God's creation is essentially good, and every bit of it came into being because he intended it to be. Obviously, this is not just an assessment of the world around us; it is a profound confirmation of the meaning of life. Because God has intended for each human being to exist, there is the built-in assurance that every life is valuable to him.

Moreover, we take seriously the biblical assertion that God has made humanity "after his own image," so that we have the possibility of communion with him. Not only has he brought us into being by his power; he has also established the prospect for a constant relationship with him. Our "chief end," as the Shorter Catechism so beautifully and simply describes it, "is to glorify God, and to enjoy him forever."

The second word that needs to be said about human nature is not nearly so attractive, though, because it has to do with our dereliction from the plan God has established. This is what we mean by the word "sin." The essential element in our sinfulness is self-centeredness or pride. Our human problem, as seen in the Reformed tradition, is that we have fallen into the sort of self-idolatry which entices us to glorify and enjoy ourselves instead of God as the chief employment of our lives. It is this state of affairs to which our forebears referred when they spoke of "total depravity."

As we have already seen, this term was not originally intended to imply that each of us is as bad as he or she can possibly be. It means rather that there is no aspect of our personhood which is exempt from the sort of distortion of God's image which takes place in our self-centered lives. Not all of us become absolute beasts in our sinfulness, but there is no aspect of our existence which has not been tainted by our selfishness.

And the worst part of this situation of human depravity is that there is no way—humanly speaking—in which this situation can be reversed. Our consciences are too marred to know goodness completely, and our wills are too marred to do the good, even if we knew it. Thus the cycle of selfishness is self-perpetuating. Any one who doubts this needs only to try to do a thoroughly unselfish deed, and then reflect with honesty upon the reasons which lay behind the act! Once we learn the fascination of the first person singular, human pride is thoroughly entrenched.

The initiative for a change in this depravity, according to our Reformed view of doctrine, belongs entirely to God. It begins, as we have seen, with his act of election. It continues into his "effectual calling" of those whom he has chosen into renewed communion with him. By God's act we are both justified (made righteous) and sanctified (set apart for spiritual growth). This latter concept is yet another basic emphasis of our theology, which is central to a proper understanding of the Christian life.

The Christian Life

The salvation which is initiated by God in the lives of the elect is an action which has discernable impact upon their behavior. It has been an important aspect of Reformed theology to seek to describe and understand the changes that begin to take place in the lives of believers.

A primary evidence of God's election, according to Calvin and his successors, is a sincere and thorough attitude of repentance. Not only are believers sorry for actions which are against God's purposes for life, they also establish firm and permanent intentions to make changes for the better. In humility and gratitude, Christians determine to strive toward the fulfillment of God's will in day to day terms.

This ongoing process is the experience to which we refer as "sanctification." It is defined in the Shorter Catechism as "the work of God's free grace whereby we are renewed in the whole man after the image of God, and are enabled more and more to die unto sin and live unto righteousness." In contrast to some other religious traditions, we Presbyterians have never held that this is a process which can be brought to completion in the present life. Thus we are not *perfectionists*.

But we do hold that it is a process of growth which, once begun by God's grace, will not be undone, either by God or by any other power.

This, of course, is one implication of the concept to which we have already made reference by the term "perseverance of the saints." Once God has chosen, he will not forsake his choice, but will continue to work out his salvation in the individual biographies of the elect.

For their part, those who are chosen will strive to attune their lives to God's will. In this effort, they will be assisted by their attentiveness to the direction of Scripture. We have always agreed with other Christians that the law of God in Scripture is there both to give order to his creation and to show the sinful how far short they fall in their quest for authentic righteousness. We have also emphasized, however, that there is a third use of the law which is even more significant in the Christian life. This is the use of the law as a guide or directive to Christian behavior—not as a *means* of gaining God's grace, but as a thanksgiving for grace already received, with no strings attached. We believe that the guidance of Scripture can provide us with the necessary guidelines for our thoughts and actions as those who are always in the process of "growing up to perfection."

Thus the Christian life becomes a life of self-imposed discipline, both in our individual experience and in the decisions and actions of the community of faith. God's love for us in Christ provides the incentive for patterns of behavior which demonstrate that love to others. Through the centuries, Calvinists have lived by the conviction that there ought to be a discernable difference in the "walk and conversation" of the elect, and we have set for ourselves the daily task of showing what that difference is, by dedicating our talents and energies to the proper service of God.

One important aspect of this belief in the discipline and employment of our God-given capacities has been the emphasis which we have traditionally placed upon the life of the mind. We believe that the disciplined use of intellect is a very important feature of Christian living. The great contribution of our tradition to higher education is both symptom and result of this commitment. We believe that every Presbyterian is a theologian, like it or not; and it has been our intention to provide the opportunity for competence in *thinking* about God, as well as in other avenues of service.

The Importance of the Community of Faith

Among the many possible aspects of the Presbyterian heritage which might be mentioned in a chapter such as this, there is one more which can by no means be omitted. It is the significance of the church as both a cause and an effect in the life of faith. It would be a very difficult thing for a Presbyterian to say that it is possible for people to be Christians by themselves. To a considerable degree, the faith of the individual is dependent upon the faith of the community. No one of us would be in the church today, had it not been for faithful parents, teachers, or friends who nurtured us; and where those people have touched our lives, the church was there, with or without buildings, sermons, and the rest. Thus, when we talk about the church, we are talking about the *context* of our own salvation.

We are also talking about a community which is not bounded by the immediate constrictions of time and space. We are a part of a community which stretches far beyond our vision, not only into the past, but into the future as well. In our present circumstances—the local congregation, the denomination, the phase of development in which we are given to live—we are both heirs and ancestors. Every time a baby is baptized in our congregation, we are given a glimpse of the future of the Christian community.

The evidence, or "marks," of the existence of this community have usually been identified in our tradition as the pure preaching and hearing the Word of God and the proper administration of the sacraments. Wherever those things are happening, the church exists; and it is incumbent upon those whom God has chosen to be a part of that community.

The Future of Presbyterianism

We began this book by saying that ours is a time in which we have happily moved from emphasizing denominational distinctiveness to seeking ways in which Christian communities of varying backgrounds and traditions can work and worship together. As we look back from this vantage over the heritage of our own tradition, the question quite naturally arises: What will be the future of the Presbyterian way? What will become of our church as we move toward a future which mixes promises and challenges for the Christian community in tantalizing fashion?

In part, the answer is up to us. We are heirs of a tradition which has proven its worth in providing a human—and usually humane—way of life for its adherents. It has successfully mixed faithfulness to a tradition with openness to new things that God does in his world. We will have the opportunity to live out that tradition in the futures that he will provide henceforth, just as those who have gone before have done.

In a much larger way, though, the answer is entirely out of our hands. The only future that we know is God's future. As Presbyterians, as Christians, as creatures of his design and intention—we shall meet him there with confidence and gratitude, in the sure knowledge that he will yet shed more light upon our way.

INDEX